THE ROARING '20s
AT THE JERSEY SHORE

4880 Lower Valley Road Atglen, Pennsylvania 19310
Printed in China

KAREN L. SCHNITZSPAHN

**I dedicate this book to the memory of my maternal grandparents,
Herb and Nell B.,
and my paternal grandparents,
Ruth and Melvin H.
who all loved the Jersey shore,
not only in the 1920s but for many years to follow.
And in loving remembrance of my parents,
Douglas and Eleanor
(who changed her first name to "Kari" in the 1940s).
If it weren't for their meeting on the Atlantic City Boardwalk, I'd wouldn't be here!**

Shore Romance. In 1936, the author's parents, Doug and Eleanor, pose in front of The Studio Cottage in Margate where they had stayed with their parents since the '20s.

Miss Margate? In 1961, the author is in front of The Studio Cottage wearing a "Miss Margate" banner (every female who stayed there got to wear it for a photo!).

Other Schiffer Books by Karen L. Schnitzspahn:
Stars of the New Jersey Shore: A Theatrical History

Covers and book designed by: Bruce Waters
Type set in Exoto Md BT-heading font/text font Aldine 721BT

ISBN: 978-0-7643-3218-0
Printed in China

The photographs, postcards, and memorabilia shown are from the author's personal collection unless otherwise credited.

Schiffer Books are available at special discounts for bulk purchases for sales promotions or premiums. Special editions, including personalized covers, corporate imprints, and excerpts can be created in large quantities for special needs. For more information contact the publisher:

Published by Schiffer Publishing Ltd.
4880 Lower Valley Road
Atglen, PA 19310
Phone: (610) 593-1777; Fax: (610) 593-2002
E-mail: Info@schifferbooks.com

For the largest selection of fine reference books on this and related subjects, please visit our web site at **www.schifferbooks.com**
We are always looking for people to write books on new and related subjects. If you have an idea for a book please contact us at the above address.

This book may be purchased from the publisher.
Include $5.00 for shipping.
Please try your bookstore first.
You may write for a free catalog.

In Europe, Schiffer books are distributed by
Bushwood Books
6 Marksbury Ave.
Kew Gardens
Surrey TW9 4JF England
Phone: 44 (0) 20 8392-8585; Fax: 44 (0) 20 8392-9876
E-mail: info@bushwoodbooks.co.uk
Website: www.bushwoodbooks.co.uk
Free postage in the U.K., Europe; air mail at cost.

CONTENTS

ACKNOWLEDGEMENTS

One of the best things about writing books is getting to know and work with extraordinary people. I am indebted to a number of them. First, I recognize distinguished New Jersey author and historian, Randall Gabrielan. His sharing of information and illustrations is invaluable, and his camaraderie is greatly appreciated. I admire his ability to follow through on a large volume of writing projects, all with great detail and exactness.

Grateful appreciation is extended to Allen "Boo" Pergament, an Atlantic City historian, for his time and effort in researching information and reviewing the accuracy of caption material for most of the Atlantic City items in this book and for allowing me to reproduce illustrations from his outstanding collection. It's been a pleasure to work with "Boo" who is very knowledgeable and has such great enthusiasm for Atlantic City's history. My heartfelt thanks go out to "Boo" and to Marlene.

A big thank you goes to Vicki Gold Levi, well-known Atlantic City historian and author, for her kindness and help. Vicki's accomplishments are multifold and she does it all with grace and style. Thank you also to Margaret Thomas Buchholz, an exceptional author who writes so beautifully about many aspects of Jersey shore history. My sincere appreciation goes to one of my favorite artists, Dick LaBonté, and to Anne LaBonté Neff for all her kindness. I always enjoy visiting the Anchor & Palette Gallery, the home of LaBonté's work in Bay Head.

I'd like to extend special thanks to Richard Sorrell Ph.D., Professor of History, Brookdale Community College, Lincroft, NJ, for his excellent comments. Thanks also to Mary Christian for her friendship and encouragement. I'm grateful, as ever, to Jane Eigenrauch of the Red Bank Public Library. Thank you to Heather Halpin of The Atlantic City Public Library, Alexandra Ford of the Ocean City Historical Museum, Lynn Eaton of Duke University Library and to Mr. David Maxwell. I extend special thanks to Virginia Richmond of The Township of Ocean Historical Museum, and to Ray Chase and the InfoAge Science-History Center at Camp Evans. Thank you to Henrietta Shelton of the Chicken Bone Beach Foundation, Atlantic City; Eric Reid of the Seaview Marriott, Galloway Twp.,NJ; Jason Ingram, General Manager of the Hollywood Golf Club, Deal; Eric Greenberg of Congress Hall, Cape May; and William Coxey of the West Jersey Chapter, National Railway Historical Society.

I'd also like to take this opportunity to recognize the knowledgeable and friendly postcard and memorabilia dealers including Barbara Booz, John Rhody, Glenn Vogel, Jim Lindemuth, and others who I always enjoy seeing at the local postcard and memorabilia shows. My appreciation also goes to fellow writer and history enthusiast Art Scott for his friendship.

Thanks to my husband Leon for his love, for his technical help, and for listening to my constant chatter about the Roaring '20s! I'm grateful to my family and thankful for my kids and grandkids – Doug, Radha, Isa, and Kieran, Greg (Max) and Erin too.

I want to applaud two people I previously co-authored books with. First, my history pal Sandra Epstein - friends like Sandy are to be treasured! And last but certainly not least, I am forever indebted to the eminent Monmouth County author and historian, George H. Moss Jr., my mentor and friend of many years. I could never have done all of this without his encouragement. Thanks George, from "Lucy!"

PREFACE

In the 1920s, two families - one in central New Jersey and one in upstate New York - eagerly prepared for their summer vacations. They loaded bulging leather suitcases containing both beach gear and Sunday best into their most prized possessions, their automobiles. Roads were improving and the families could enjoy taking both gravel and paved roads to Atlantic City, although the trip would be bouncy to say the least. Before roadside diners and fast food, a jug of drinking water and a picnic basket were essential.

The "war to end all wars" was over. People felt that they deserved to enjoy themselves. Optimism and prosperity seemed to dominate the mood of Americans, but a dark side loomed beneath the surface of the Roaring '20s. And yet, these families were probably not attuned to that. Their exposure to the world was from what they read in the newspapers, and then through the new at-home marvel, radio. Their main concerns were earning a living, staying healthy, raising their children, and coping with the changing lifestyle of the postwar era. The jaunts to the seashore might be the only trips they'd take in the 1920s.

The upstate New York family lived in Niagara Falls, a tourist site, but they relished the seashore. Mr. B., a chemist, had worked with explosives during the war but now he was working on developing a new kind of soap. Mrs. B., a former school teacher, was a stay-at-home mom. Not fond of the new flapper look, she tucked her hair back tightly under a hairnet and wore plain outdated, ankle-length dresses. Sadly, their first baby, a boy named Herbert, died in infancy during the 1918 flu epidemic. In 1920, their daughter was born and they named her Eleanor. She was my mother. My maternal grandparents drove to the Jersey shore to enjoy some fun with their little girl, but the loss of their son haunted them. They would not have any more children.

The central New Jersey family lived in South River, a small town with light industry in Middlesex County. Dr. H., a physician, had recently established his general practice after interning and working in Newark, New Jersey.

His new office was attached to the family's house on a tree-lined residential street. Many of his treatments were natural and homeopathic. He often said how he believed that sea bathing was like a healthful tonic. Mrs. H. was his office assistant and took care of nursing duties, though she was not not licensed. A gifted pianist, she had given up on the idea of music career. They had two sons. Douglas was born in 1918 during the height of the devastating flu epidemic. He was my father. His younger brother, Melvin, was born in the early '20s. Mrs. H., though a devoted mother and homemaker, was intrigued by the new freedoms that women were gaining. In 1920, she had her long auburn hair snipped off and made into a switch. Her short, marceled style would stay with her until she passed away in the 1970s.

At the Jersey shore, the two sides of my family frolicked in the waves and strolled on the boardwalk. They sipped lemonade, chewed salt water taffy, and gawked at all sorts of freaky entertainment. They didn't know each other in the 1920s. Then, in the mid-1930s after the roaring subsided and during the Great Depression, my father and mother met by chance on the Atlantic City Boardwalk. The two good-looking teenagers, each vacationing there with their families, as they had done for over a decade, fell in love at first sight. How romantic can you get? They married a few years later. I was their only child. Today, I'm told they were two of thousands who met and fell in love on the Boardwalk.

By the Sea. In 1924, Mr. and Mrs. B. and daughter Eleanor are at a New Jersey beach.

Driving Down the Shore. Dr. and Mrs. H., their sons and Mrs. H.'s mother are in their automobile ready to head for Atlantic City c.1928.

Little Eleanor. The author's mother enjoys an ice cream cone at the shore in 1925.

A Roadside Stop. The Doctor's family poses for a photo by a roadside well on the way down the shore, c.1928.

A Decade of Contrasts

"The Jazz Age"

flappers

the Charleston

mass-produced flivvers

The Great Gatsby

radio broadcasts

America's Sweetheart, Mary Pickford

rumrunners

speakeasies

Turkish cigarettes

Mah Jong

gold diggers

flagpole sitting

"The Sultan of Swat," Babe Ruth

hip flasks

Ain't We Got Fun

art deco

"the cat's meow"

marathon dancing

Highlights

These are some of the popular phrases, people, and things commonly associated with the debauchedly-regarded decade from 1919-1929 known as The Roaring '20s:

Events of the 1920s that made national headlines, to name a few, included:

The Teapot Dome Scandal when government officials got rich on stolen Navy oil

The Boston Police Strike

the execution of Sacco and Vanzetti

"Lucky Lindy's" non-stop New York to Paris flight

the Hall-Mills murder case (New Jersey)

The Scopes Monkey Trial

Al "Scarface" Capone and the Chicago St. Valentines' Day Massacre

"Black Tuesday," when the 1929 stock market crashed

The Roaring '20s was that remarkable period wedged between the close of the First World War and the beginning of the Great Depression. It was wild and crazy, footloose, and fancy-free. It was dark and corrupt, progressive yet prejudiced. There are notable differences between the early twenties and the later twenties, with the legendary good times really starting after Calvin Coolidge became president in 1923. So, what made those years "roar?"

The Mood of the Nation

A feeling of euphoria existed as the soldiers gradually returned home from Europe after the Great War. A centenarian named Edwina Hazzard recalled for this author (in a 2003 interview) a memorable train ride from New York City on November 7th, 1918, to Red Bank, New Jersey. She was going to visit her family for an autumn weekend at their Jersey shore summer home. The conductor announced that the war was over! She described how people were cheering, singing, and dancing in the aisles, but it was a false alarm. The real armistice came four days later on November 11th. Hooray! The "war to end all wars" had really ended. The world would be a better place...or would it?

At the beginning of the 1920s, there was optimism and rising prosperity, but feelings of fear and uncertainty loomed beneath the surface. A mood of ultraconservatism prevailed and many citizens rejected President Woodrow Wilson's League of Nations. Right wingers worried about too many immigrants coming to America. Frederick Lewis Allen describes in *Only Yesterday*, his 1931 book about the 1920s, how an extreme fear of Bolsheviks affected many Americans at the dawn of the '20s. Allen calls it "The Big Red Scare."

Welcome Home! Soldiers returning from the Great War in 1919 are marching in a parade at Red Bank.
Collection of the Red Bank Public Library.

ENTER THE FLAPPERS

Women got the vote with the ratification of the Nineteenth Amendment in 1920, bobbed their hair, and raised their hemlines. The word "flapper" is used to describe the new woman after the World War who abandoned corsets and wore low-waisted dresses with straight lines. Usually described as daring and outspoken, the flapper drank, smoked cigarettes, and danced the night away. There seem to be many explanations for the origin of the word flapper and some attribute it to the boots young women wore that were not fastened and flapped as they walked. At the New Jersey beaches, flappers wore the latest form-fitting one piece bathing suits that were often "ticketed" by official beach censors.

Women had learned to be more self-sufficient while the men were overseas. Now more women entered the workforce than ever before, but they still had far to go in their struggle for equality. Most of the jobs for women were clerical and it was hard to secure management positions. Women were still expected to cook, clean, and take care of the kids but they had new appliances and products to make life easier including electric vacuum cleaners and irons, boxed Betty Crocker™ cake mixes, and even packaged LaChoy™ Chinese food.

The Roaring '20s represented a new morality and more openness about sexuality. Automobile dates gave young couples the chance to be alone, instead of the traditional parlor courtships of their parents' time. Also, homosexuality became more acceptable during the 1920s, although attitudes towards same sex relationships would regress in the next decade. Positive changes were happening for some people but not for others. For African Americans, things hadn't changed much as there was still widespread segregation, both formal and informal. Many white people were fascinated with the new jazz and dancing that originated in black communities, but otherwise did not accept blacks into their social sphere. African Americans were not welcome at Jersey shore beaches and boardwalks, and were seated in separate sections at theaters.

Chic Flappers. A group of young women look fabulous in the latest fashions at the Atlantic City Boardwalk on Easter Sunday 1923. *Vicki Gold Levi Collection.*

"THE NOBLE EXPERIMENT"

The Anti-Saloon League, Women's Christian Temperance Union, and other groups fought for many years to ban alcoholic beverages. They believed the "demon rum" to be the cause of corruption, wife beatings, child abuse, and murder. They weren't the only ones who wanted America to go dry. Many factory employers were concerned about the effects of drinking on their workers' productivity. Others worried about health problems related to alcohol, and many of those fears were certainly not unfounded.

The anti-drinkers wish came true when at midnight, January 16, 1920, national prohibition became a reality and the United States went legally dry. The 18th Amendment to the US Constitution, ratified in 1919, established Prohibition by making the sale or manufacture of alcohol illegal. The Volstead Act that was passed on October 28, 1919, made it clear that any beverage that was more than 0.5% alcohol by volume (including beer, wine, and malt liquor) was prohibited.

A large number of American working class folk were accustomed to moderately drinking spirits as part of their regular diet, especially the populations of recent European immigrants. Ritzy socialites found it hard to think of life without cocktails, and the common working man would miss the relaxation afforded by his neighborhood tavern. The World War had helped make a good case for the advocates of prohibition. It was said that grain should be used to make bread for the soldiers, not whiskey. Anti-German movements fueled the fire to shut down breweries that were mostly run by Germans. "Near beer" was allowed but to make it, you had to make real beer and then take the alcohol out.

BOOTLEGGERS AND RUMRUNNERS

The biggest problem with prohibition was that it was unenforceable. The New Jersey coast was one of the most active places in the United States for the illegal smuggling of "hooch." Hundreds of people died in "bootlegging wars" along the Atlantic coast and US borders while the US Coast Guard did its best to do their job of stopping the unlawful trafficking. Foreign ships, from such diverse destinations as Great Britain and Cuba would hang out along the "rum line" three miles off the Atlantic coast and wait for the small local boats to sneak out after dark to gather the forbidden bottles. In 1924, the line was moved, by an act of Congress, to twelve miles making it tough for the local bootleggers, many of whom were ordinary citizens with small boats who needed to make some money for their families. Sometimes the Coast Guard cutters would intercept them, but perhaps more often than not, the local bootleggers made it back to the shore with their valuable goods. The rum-runners worked up and down the entire Jersey coast. Some of the busiest areas were around Sandy Hook and Atlantic City but more remote locations such as Long Beach Island and the waters off Cape May County also had much illicit activity. The legendary Captain William McCoy, based in Florida, operated a big fleet of ships that would hover along "Rum Row." His trusted cheer became known as "the real McCoy." McCoy did get caught once off the coast at Sea Bright and served jail time in New Jersey.

On the Rum Line. "The liquor-laden British schooner *M.M. Gardner* is off the New Jersey Coast. April 1, 1923." *The United States Coast Guard.*

LIQUOR-LADEN SCHOONER OFF N.J. COAST. 4-19-23

Illegal Booze. A motor boat is making contact with the liquor laden British schooner *Katharine* off the New Jersey Coast. *The United States Coast Guard.*

DETECTIVE SMITH · MAYOR BAMFORD REV.HANEY · OFFICER LOKERSON

Results of A Raid. Detective Smith, Belmar Mayor William Bamford, Reverend Haney, and Officer Lokerson pose with liquor bottles they confiscated from bootleggers in 1923. *Courtesty of Dennis Lewis.*

Illegal bars, known as speakeasies, were prevalent, especially along the New Jersey coast. The usual connotation is of someone knocking on a little window and whispering "Joe sent me." The cry of "Raid!" was heard as police stormed illegal watering holes, and yet backs were often turned or bribes were taken. Most people who drank found that they could continue to drink and those who would never think of breaking laws previously did so with few qualms during prohibition. The farms and wooded areas near the coast of New Jersey, such as those in the Pine Barrens, concealed stills for illegal moonshine and remote places for gangsters to dispose of bodies.

Concealed hip flasks became popular items and the image of a sassy flapper pulling up her skirt to reveal a flask strapped to her leg remains an indelible sign of the times. Physicians could legally write prescriptions for consumable alcohol, for medicinal use only. As a result, plenty of people surely feigned maladies that would require an alcoholic remedy. On the other hand, certain communities along the New Jersey coast were not affected by prohibition and even welcomed it. For instance, Ocean City was founded in the 19th century by Methodist ministers as a dry, healthful resort and the town was unaffected by the change in the law. Ocean City remains dry to this day.

"The Fiery Summons"

In the early 1920s, the Ku Klux Klan exerted a strong presence in New Jersey. Its "fiery summons" as proclaimed on their handouts was heard most loudly at the shore, especially in Monmouth and Ocean counties, although it was also active in the northern industrial areas and various counties throughout the state. The KKK, with its hateful origins in the post-Civil War South, lingered quietly for years but a newly organized Klan was revived in 1915. The hooded order proclaimed itself as a native born, white, Anglo-Saxon Protestant group opposed to "Catholics, Jews, and Negroes." The membership came mostly from working class laborers but pillars of the community including local professionals, police officers, politicians and ministers donned hoods and joined the ranks. The organization was not known to be as violent in New Jersey as in some other states; nevertheless they terrorized and threatened the targets of their wrath, mostly Catholics at the Jersey shore. The Klan membership names were kept secret but an estimated 7,000 Jersey shore residents belonged in the early 1920s. The New Jersey Klan was legally organized in 1923 with the state headquarters located at the former Marconi wireless station in Wall Township. Some of the KKK's meeting places were known as "pleasure clubs."

The Konclave. This is the cover of a July 4, 1924 souvenir program for the huge Tri-State gathering of the KKK held at Elkwood Park, Oceanport. *Moss Archives.*

Klan Parking Lot. A huge number of autos were parked adjacent to Elkwood Park (now the site of Monmouth Park Racetrack) for the 1924 KKK Konclave. Klan members brought their families with them for the event. *Collection of Randall Gabrielan.*

In June of 1924, the Klan leased the resort-like property then known as Elkwood Park at Long Branch (the site of today's Monmouth Park Racetrack, Oceanport) and a few weeks later held a huge "Tri-State Klonvocation" there that was said to be attended by more than 20,000 Klansmen and their families. In June of 1924, the Klan leased the resort-like property then known as Elkwood Park at Long Branch (the site of today's Monmouth Park Racetrack, Oceanport) and a few weeks later held a huge "Tri-State Klonvocation" there that was said to be attended by more than 20,000 Klansmen and their families. The main purpose of the conference was to protest the possibility of New York's Alfred E. Smith, an Irish Catholic, as Democratic nominee for President of the United States. Smith was being considered, but ultimately John Davis was nominated. At the close of the festivities, some 4,000 hooded members marched from Elkwood Park, through Oceanport, and down Broadway in Long Branch. According to *Entertaining A Nation, The Career of Long Branch (WPA 1940)*, the effect of the march on business was a disaster. "The Jewish summer residents departed from the town the next day practically en masse, leaving a deserted city of ruined shopkeepers and empty hotels and boardinghouses. The Negro population locked its doors tight and refused to emerge on the streets for several days. Similarly, Catholics, for whose benefit several fiery crosses had been burned; either left the community or took steps to protect themselves…"

By 1925, the Klan had diminished at the Jersey shore as many of its supporters began to come to their senses and realize the futility of racism and hate, as well as the economic consequences. Some Klan activities persisted into the 1930s, but a growing tolerance and recognition of religious pluralism helped to crush the Klan's influence.

KKK Vehicle. A hooded Klan member can be seen next to a motor vehicle that is decorated for the KKK's parade at the 1924 Konclave. *Collection of Randall Gabrielan.*

CULTURAL RENAISSANCE

One of the best things about the post World War I era was the surge of creative inspiration in art, music, and literature. During the Roaring '20s, a cultural revolution took place in America, the likes of which would not be seen again until the 1960s. With the great migration of blacks from the rural South to the industrial Northeast, came a new culture. The "Harlem Renaissance" was born and talented black writers and musicians found a way to thrive despite the racial bigotry of the '20s.

Although it was "the jazz age," traditional brass band concerts were still heard at the piers and bandstands as they had been since the 19th century. Opera was well-liked and people adored the great operatic and classical stars, many of whom visited the New Jersey shore. Pop music of the decade included tunes like *Ain't She Sweet*, *Button Up Your Overcoat*, *I'm Sitting on Top of the World*, and novelties such as Hawaiian songs strummed on ukuleles. However, some of the most exciting music to come out of the Roaring '20s was heard secretly. It traveled from New Orleans and the dance halls of Chicago. The rhythmic sounds were played by black musicians in the speakeasies, smoky road houses, and clubs on "the other side of the tracks" in neighborhoods where African Americans and immigrants who worked at low-level service jobs at the resorts lived. During the 1920s, African American stars emerged such as Bessie Smith, Louis Armstrong, Duke Ellington, and Count Basie ("The Kid from Red Bank"). Jazz would endure and become more prominent during the 1930s and beyond.

Modernism in art and architecture that started to unfold in the first decade of the 20th century was in full bloom during the 1920s. Abstract expressionism, surrealism and Dadaism were attracting attention. Clean, modern lines in architecture replaced the Beaux Arts look and sleek skyscrapers began to rise. Photography reached new heights as an art form. Many of the ground-breaking creative trends spread to the New Jersey shore because of its proximity to New York and Philadelphia.

Despite censorship initiated by moral conservatives, provocative literature and films managed to flourish during the era. Much literature that continues to be read and enjoyed today was first published in the Roaring '20s. The novels of F. Scott Fitzgerald, Sinclair Lewis, and D.H. Lawrence, Gertrude Stein, Ernest Hemingway; the poetry of black writer Langston Hughes and plays by Eugene O'Neill all came out of the 1920s.

The New Jersey shore was home to some outstanding writers associated with the Roaring '20s including Dorothy Parker who was born Dorothy Rothschild in West End, NJ, on August 22, 1893. Parker had a reputation for her cutting witticisms and one of the most quoted lines from her poetry is "Men seldom make passes at girls who wear glasses." She was well known for her short stories, many of which first appeared in *The New Yorker*, and she was a regular member of the celebrated literary "Round Table" at Manhattan's Algonquin Hotel in the 1920s. Parker died in 1967, but her writings remain popular and events are held today commemorating her including a "Dorothy Parker Day" at Long Branch. The great American writer and literary critic Edmund Wilson was born in Red Bank, NJ, in 1895. An unfinished work at the time of his death in 1972 was *The Twenties*, a compilation of his journals that included some entries about the Jersey coast.

Birthplace of Dorothy Parker. A plaque commemorates the site of the house where the witty author was born (now an apartment complex) on August 22, 1893, in West End (Long Branch) New Jersey.

DOROTHY PARKER

A portrait of young Dorothy Parker. Library of Congress

Before Television, Malls, and Disneyland

People were moving from rural areas to the cities during the 1920s. And yet urbanization was the trend that led to workers needing vacations to get away from the cities especially during the oppressive summer heat. The New Jersey shore provided an ideal place, especially convenient for New Yorkers and Philadelphians, to enjoy cool breezes and salt water bathing as well as a variety of amusements. Homes and apartments were not yet air conditioned and ocean breezes were more satisfying than electric fans. Besides, people wanted to get out en masse and be entertained. As they began to have more home entertainment with the rise of radio during this era, public entertainment venues would lose some business but for the most part, the piers and theaters at shore resorts attracted huge crowds during the Roaring '20s. The movies became an obsession, especially with the advent of talkies in 1927.

The New Jersey shore resorts provided much for both the wealthy and the middle class visitors. Some thirty years before Disneyland and suburban malls opened, the New Jersey boardwalks of the 1920s offered a fantasy world of entertainment, shopping, and excitement. The rich and famous who stayed at the luxury hotels, strolled the boards in their pricey duds and furs alongside hardworking recent immigrants who dusted off their Sunday best, but African Americans were excluded from the picture in the 1920s.

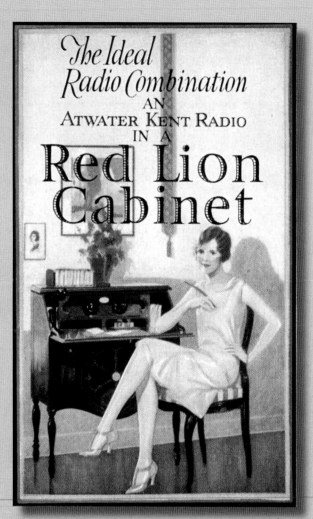

On the Radio. Sales of radios soared after the first home broadcasts in 1922. This ad brochure from a Monmouth County radio store features a lovely flapper with a state-of-the-art 1920s desk radio.

The Great Outdoors

Besides the resort cities with boardwalks and hotels, many miles along the New Jersey coast were open lands and barren sand dunes at this time though improved roads and bridges would unite them with the rest of civilization considerably by the middle of the 1930s. The rustic and swampy areas did attract certain tourists – the fisherman, duck hunters, gunners, and campers who enjoyed the great outdoors. Fortunately, there were some individuals and groups who realized the importance of conservation and without them; we would not have those precious coastal areas that are undeveloped and preserved for wildlife today. Many people became increasingly aware of beaches wearing away in the '20s. Beach erosion was dramatically evident at Long Beach Island. In 1927, the Little Egg Harbor Lighthouse that stood on the north end of Tucker's Island fell into the sea. The coastline was, and is, constantly changing.

Storms, hurricanes and nor'easters, as well as flooding and blizzards, were of course, a constant worry at Jersey shore resorts. Although the 1920s had its share of bad storms, there was nothing during the decade as devastating as those that would slam the coast in later years such as the hurricane of 1944 or the great storm of 1962. Fire was an ever-present danger especially at the old hotels, and fire departments along the Jersey coast kept busy, most of them manned by hard-working volunteers. In reminiscing about the 1920s, Eleanor Hardy-Vogt, a former summer resident of Ocean Grove who watched the North

End Hotel ablaze said: "A good fire was considered great entertainment. People in all states of dress and undress would pile into their cars and head for the spot. You had to go and see these things for yourself – no television for an instant replay." (*Asbury Park Press*, May 26, 1985.)

Green Beaches. At Ocean City, an unidentified group of environmentalists is planting beach grass to help protect the dunes in the 1920s. ©*Ocean City Historical Museum, Inc.*

TAKING A LOOK BACK

This book takes a look at tourism during the 1920s through postcards and photographs from the author's collection as well as other private collections and those of several libraries and museums. Most of the available 1920s material illustrates the best of times enjoyed by the wealthy and middle class vacationers with few images of either the hard-working minorities or of the gangsters and the vice. The bulk of the material consists of postcards, promotional booklets, tourist photos, and advertisements. A good number of Jersey shore locations are included, but difficult choices had to be made based on availability and time. There is so much more, but it's impossible to include everything! My concentration became the coastal resorts from Sandy Hook to Cape May although a few towns further inland and in the Bayshore area are represented.

As I began to compile these illustrations, I realized how complex the Roaring '20s were. The decade roared for some, but not for others. It is only in retrospect that we can see flaws more clearly, and someday the contrasts of our own "modern" times will be observed by the next generations. May the reader find this book to be "the bee's knees" and most of all, an insightful journey back in time.

A Sea of People. Each year, photos like this were taken of the huge crowd on the Atlantic City Boardwalk for the Easter Parade. This one is from 1922. *Collection of Allen "Boo" Pergament.*

THE AUTOMOBILE AGE

In the late 1890s, the "horseless carriage" made its entrance and wealthy vacationers purchased electric vehicles. The most talked about owner of an "electric" (in fact six of them!) was "Diamond Jim" Brady. He made a legendary ride in his specially designed electric Brougham with the gorgeous star Lillian Russell on Ocean Avenue at Long Branch. It wasn't long before gasoline-powered motor cars entered the marketplace and were snapped up by the well-heeled shore cottagers. A whole new world had opened up. Touring in automobiles became a popular type of recreation for visitors to the coast in the early years of the twentieth century.

Although some people insisted that the automobile craze wouldn't last and nothing could replace the trusty horse, a new economy was evolving. As blacksmiths and livery stables lost business, gasoline stations and auto garages were opening up. As automakers improved their products and demand lowered the prices, more middle-class people purchased them. Henry Ford's Model T, known at first as the "Tin Lizzie" and later as a "flivver" was produced from 1908-1927. It was the first affordable mass-produced automobile and cost around $300. In 1927, the Model T was replaced by the Model A.

Many of the New Jersey shore roads were dirt or gravel and good paved roads became as important as the autos themselves. Bridges and causeways were also critical to travel, and the openings of these improvements were causes for celebrations. It was not until the 1930s and the WPA projects during the Great Depression that better bridges and highway projects were constructed, many of them still in use, or just being replaced today.

At the beginning of the 1920s, most visitors to the New Jersey coast still came by train, but autos could be seen everywhere! Steamboats still carried passengers to shore points as the ride was a pleasant excursion. New, streamlined and faster trains appeared around the end of the 1920s, but then declined due to the increase of automobiles and air travel. Trolleys provided local transportation in many shore towns but began to diminish and were replaced by bus lines in the early 1930s.

Besides rough roads, there were additional problems for the automobile owners in the '20s. Gasoline was not expensive, but often hard to find. "Ford" was mockingly said to mean "Fix or Repair Daily." Frequent flat tires, always upsetting, were a huge problem, as were other needed repairs. Despite everything, the automobile gave the driver a sense of ownership and privacy that could not be beat.

In the '20s, small airplanes began transporting tourists and were used for sightseeing. The airplane was the upcoming means of commercial transportation and by the close of the 1920s; new airfields were opening in New Jersey. Rigid airships were in use for overseas journeys in the late '20s but would come to an abrupt halt in 1937 with the crash of the Hindenburg at Lakehurst. And yet, air travel would continue to develop and to lure people away from the Jersey shore to faraway places.

STEAMBOAT LANDING, RED BANK, N. J.

STEAMER CITY OF KEANSBURG LEAVING BATTERY, N. Y. FOR KEANSBURG, N. J.

106

Steamboat Landing. From the early 1800s until the early 1930s, Red Bank on the North Shrewsbury River (Navesink River) was a bustling port for steamboats that carried both farm produce and passengers. The *Albertina* and the *Sea Bird* were two of the well-known steamers that came here. This postcard view, c.1919 is a sign of the changing times with both an automobile and a horse drawn vehicle waiting to pick up visitors at the dock in the area of today's Marine Park.

City of Keansburg. In 1926, after the steamer *Keansburg* was destroyed by fire, it was replaced by the *City of Keansburg*. The new state-of-the-art steamboat held 2,000 passengers and would make three round-trips daily from the Battery in New York City to its namesake town on the Bayshore of New Jersey.

CROWD LANDING AT ATLANTIC HIGHLANDS, N. J.

The Waiting Crowd. When steamboats came into the old Atlantic Highlands pier, dozens of autos would be waiting to take visitors to various destinations as this 1920s postcard illustrates. The "hack" vehicle in the front, a sort of shuttle bus, has an Asbury Park pennant on the side. Pedestrians can also been seen walking on the pier towards the mainland.

The Sandy Hook Route. Owned by the Central Railroad of New Jersey, the 260 ft. *Sandy Hook* was built in 1889 and remained in service making runs from New York City until 1943. The steamer was then used for military service and returned in 1946. But, because of a government decree that prohibited duplicate routes, *The Sandy Hook* and her sister ship *The Monmouth*, could not run because the Central Railroad trains had direct service to shore points. *The Monmouth* was scrapped in 1941, and *The Sandy Hook* went out of service in 1947. *Collection of the Red Bank Public Library.*

A Hub of Activity. The original Burlew's on Front St. in Keyport was a popular seafood restaurant and fishery. Notice the vintage bus traveling from Atlantic City on the right in this late '20s scene. Along with the rise of automobiles, more buses were being used. Buses became increasingly popular means of transportation as roads improved.

Country Roads. A postcard dated 1925 depicts a typical dirt road near the seashore resort of Bradley Beach in Monmouth County. The hills in the background must be the Shark River Hills.

Another Flat Tire! Breakdowns and flat tires were frequent occurrences in the Roaring '20s. This humorous 1920s postcard of a cute flapper has a double entendre. A "flat tire" was the jargon at the time for a dull or disappointing date.

Pilgrim Pathway. At Ocean Grove in 1923, a lone automobile is seen on the tent-lined street. Gates to this resort run by the Methodist Camp Meeting Association were closed on Sundays and cars forbidden to enter. The Sunday ban on "wheeled vehicles" was not lifted until 1980.

Jolly Travelers. In 1920, members of the Yearly family of Riverton, NJ, are joking alongside their automobile that is parked on the sand at Harvey Cedars. There is a little boy partially hidden behind the woman in the middle. Whatever is the woman at the rear of the car doing, and do you wonder what's in the thermos? *Joseph F. Yearly, courtesy of his granddaughter, Mary Flanagan.*

Where to Park? At the height of the season, in August 1925, automobiles are cruising up and down Belmar's Ocean Avenue. Many were probably looking for parking spaces. Parking meters were not yet in use. This photo, looking south, shows the high pilings that the Fifth Avenue Pavilion rested on. Eventually, the beach became even with the tops of the pilings. *Moss Archives.*

Emergency Care. Frank Mihlon Jr. stands proudly with his father, Frank Sr., who was the benefactor for this ambulance, Belmar's first. It was young Frank who, after witnessing an accident, crusaded to establish Belmar's First Aid Squad, known as the first independent squad in the United States to transport patients. With the increased automobile traffic during the '20s, this was an important contribution and other shore towns soon began their own first aid squads. With state-of-the-art equipment today, dedicated volunteer squads provide invaluable service.

Fish and Fuel. A panoramic view, looking east, of the first Beach Haven Crest Fishery gives an idea of how rustic the dirt Boulevard was in the late 1920s. Tonnes Bohn and his wife stand in front of the shack where they sold fresh fish, clams, squid, and lobsters. Customers could make one stop to fill up at the lone pump with Standard gas and to buy seafood or bait. *From "Island Album: Photographs and Memories of Long Beach Island" by Margaret Thomas Buchholz ©2006. By permission of Down The Shore Publishing.*

Take the Guess out of your "Gas" Tank

IN cold weather or hot you know just what your motor will do on a diet of "Standard" Motor Gasoline. You don't have to wonder whether she'll start promptly. You *know* she will. There's no guesswork about how far you can go on five gallons.

"Standard" Motor Gasoline doesn't just happen to be good. Scientific selection of crude oils, perfected refining processes, and tests throughout every manufacturing stage produce the uniformity and ex-

cellence of every gallon of "Standard" Motor Gasoline.

In every property that affects motor operation—volatility at low temperatures, freedom from corrosive acids, cleanness and burning qualities—"Standard" Motor Gasoline is an improved gasoline, a *balanced* motor fuel that assures the utmost economy and efficiency.

Drive in where you see the familiar "S. O." sign. Get a tankful of "Standard" Motor Gasoline to-day. Notice how quickly your car starts, how easily she takes hard hills. Measure your mileage. You'll soon take the guess out of motoring and cut the costs down.

P. S.—Good oil is fully as important as good gasoline. You can save repair bills by using POLARINE.

STANDARD OIL COMPANY
(New Jersey)

A "Diet" for Automobiles. A 1921 newspaper advertisement for Standard Oil praises the reliability of its products as a good "diet" for your auto that will cut costs down.

Drive Carefully! The auto bridge on Deal Lake, Deal Beach NJ, leading to Asbury Park is depicted on a 1920s postcard. There is no white line, only a flimsy sign in the middle saying "Keep to the Right."

AUTO BRIDGE ON DEAL LAKE, DEAL BEACH, N. J.

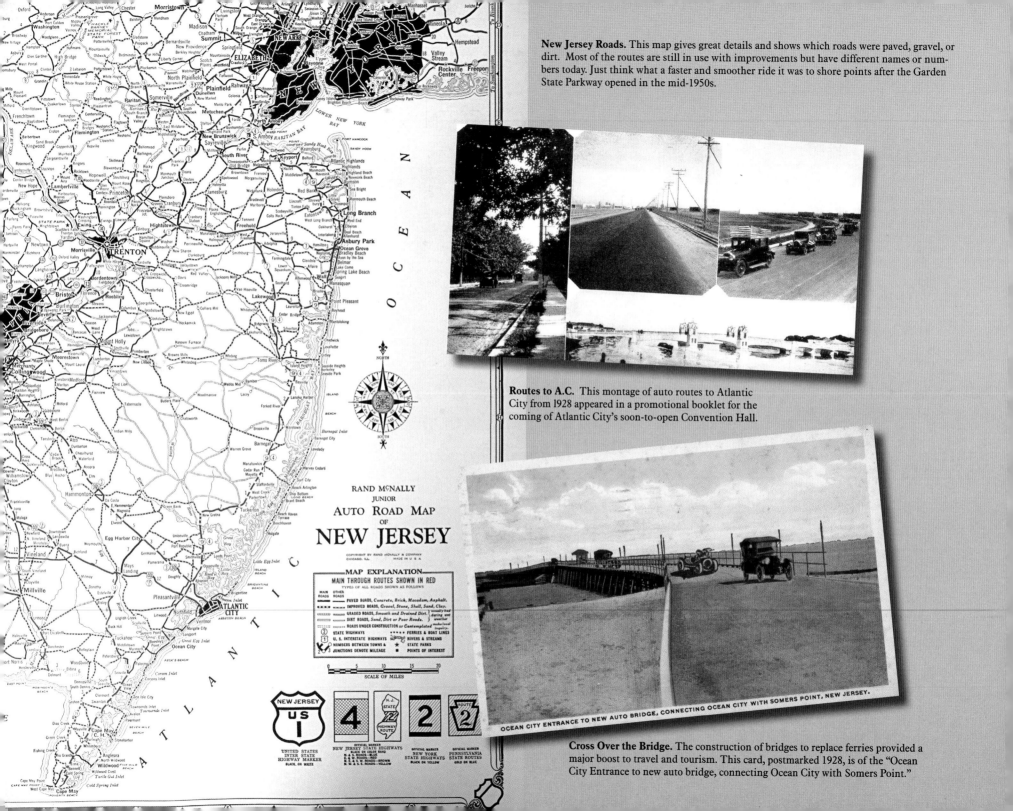

New Jersey Roads. This map gives great details and shows which roads were paved, gravel, or dirt. Most of the routes are still in use with improvements but have different names or numbers today. Just think what a faster and smoother ride it was to shore points after the Garden State Parkway opened in the mid-1950s.

Routes to A.C. This montage of auto routes to Atlantic City from 1928 appeared in a promotional booklet for the coming of Atlantic City's soon-to-open Convention Hall.

RAND McNALLY
JUNIOR
AUTO ROAD MAP
OF
NEW JERSEY

COPYRIGHT BY RAND McNALLY & COMPANY
CHICAGO, ILL.   MADE IN U.S.A.

MAP EXPLANATION
MAIN THROUGH ROUTES SHOWN IN RED
TYPES OF ALL ROADS SHOWN AS FOLLOWS

MAIN ROADS	OTHER ROADS	
		PAVED ROADS, Concrete, Brick, Macadam, Asphalt.
		IMPROVED ROADS, Gravel, Stone, Shell, Sand, Clay.
		GRADED ROADS, Smooth and Drained Dirt.
		DIRT ROADS, Sand, Dirt or Poor Roads.
		ROADS UNDER CONSTRUCTION or Contemplated

STATE HIGHWAYS
U. S. INTERSTATE HIGHWAYS
NUMBERS BETWEEN TOWNS &
JUNCTIONS DENOTE MILEAGE

FERRIES & BOAT LINES
RIVERS & STREAMS
STATE PARKS
POINTS OF INTEREST

SCALE OF MILES
0   5   10   15   20

NEW JERSEY
US 1
UNITED STATES
INTER STATE
HIGHWAY MARKER
BLACK ON WHITE

4
OFFICIAL MARKER
NEW JERSEY STATE HIGHWAYS
BLACK ON COLOR BAND
N. & S. ROADS—BLUE
E. & W. ROADS—RED
N. E. & S. W. ROADS—BROWN
N. W. & S. E. ROADS—YELLOW

N.J. STATE HIGHWAY ROUTE

2
OFFICIAL MARKER
NEW YORK
STATE HIGHWAYS
BLACK ON YELLOW

ROUTE 2
OFFICIAL MARKER
PENNSYLVANIA
STATE ROUTES
GOLD ON BLUE

OCEAN CITY ENTRANCE TO NEW AUTO BRIDGE, CONNECTING OCEAN CITY WITH SOMERS POINT, NEW JERSEY.

Cross Over the Bridge. The construction of bridges to replace ferries provided a major boost to travel and tourism. This card, postmarked 1928, is of the "Ocean City Entrance to new auto bridge, connecting Ocean City with Somers Point."

Cape May Kids. In the early 1920s, two children stand proudly by the family's Model T at their Cape May home, a small farm, only a short ride from the ocean.

Autos, Autos, Everywhere. The roads must have been congested on this day in the 1920s when all these autos converged on Cape May so their occupants could attend a band concert. For those who think today's pop concerts create traffic jams, just think of this scene!

Traveling by Train. Besides automobiles, visitors to the shore continued to use the railroads and there were plenty of trains running along the Jersey coast in the 1920s. Many of the stations were well-kept and attractive such as this one at Bradley Beach with its park like setting as seen on this 1925 postcard. Automobiles are seen waiting for a train to arrive.

The Blue Comet. Despite the growing popularity of automobiles, many travelers preferred to ride the rails and not worry about things like flat tires or finding gas. The last great luxury coach train at the Jersey shore was the legendary Blue Comet that ran from 1929-1941 between New York and Atlantic City. Many people today are familiar with the name of the Blue Comet because of episode #85 of the television series, *The Sopranos*, in which Bobby is killed while buying a model of a Blue Comet at a hobby shop. *This timetable from the train's first year is from the Heston Collection of the Atlantic City Public Library and is reproduced courtesy of the West Jersey Chapter, National Railway Historical Society.*

Look, Up in the Sky! Dirigibles were experiencing a renaissance in the 1920s. Jersey shore vacationers delighted in watching them as they would head for their landings at Lakehurst Naval Air Station. The German airship Graf Zeppelin, started its career in 1928, landed at Lakehurst, New Jersey, and made transoceanic flights to countries all over the world. In 1937, the great rigid airship Hindenberg caught on fire and crashed at Lakehurst. The tragedy, as well as political reasons, and the impending war marked the end of passenger airship travel.

DR. HUGO ECKENER

GRAF ZEPPELIN

HYDROPLANE RETURNED FROM A FLIGHT, ATLANTIC CITY, N. J.

CURTISS

The Flying Boats. A Curtiss hydroplane is pictured on this postcard from 1921. Aviation pioneer Glenn Curtiss developed these planes that were used for sightseeing tours and as a mode of travel for wealthy people. The first passenger flight between Philadelphia and Atlantic City's Inlet was on June 25, 1919 at a speed of "better than a mile a minute" and cost a dollar per minute (90 to 130 minutes depending on weather conditions). In 1922, regular daily air service on hydroplanes between the Ritz-Carlton Hotels in New York City and Atlantic City began.

CURTISS

An Artist's View of a Seaplane. A 1922 painting of a Curtiss flying boat at the Atlantic City Inlet by Henry Reuterdahl (1871-1925) provides a lively impressionistic view. Reuterdahl, a noted marine artist who lived in Weehawken, NJ, was a Lieutenant Commander in the United States Naval Reserves.

Celebrities At Bader Field. An impressive group of aviators including Amelia Earhart, Charles Lindbergh, and Eddie Rickenbacker (former WWI ace and then president of Eastern Airlines) are in this 1931 photo. Boxer Gene Tunney and Atlantic City Mayor Bacharach and his wife are also in the picture. The aircraft is a Curtiss Condor biplane. At that time, Eastern was operating Bader Field airport at Atlantic City where this photo was taken. By 1933, Eastern had moved out. Commercial air travel was growing rapidly as the Roaring '20s ended and the Great Depression began. Bader Field was in operation from 1910 – 2006. *Jack E. Boucher, Photographer and Alfred M. Heston Collection,* Atlantic City Free Public Library.

Tourists driving down the shore in the 1920s, did not find the motels that would eventually line the highways in the next few decades. However, there were some little clusters of cabins called "motor courts" that were forerunners of the later motels. Or, the hardy travelers would pitch a tent and camp out along the way. Those "doo wop" Jersey motels, in bright aqua and flamingo pink, didn't blossom until after the Second World War.

Those who planned to stay for a while could rent homes ranging from sumptuous "cottages" to little bungalows at beach towns along the Jersey coast. Most of the tiny homes had no plumbing or electricity in the early '20s but by the end of the decade, many were updated. Some families opted to stay at comfy, rambling boarding houses in the more populated areas, far cheaper than hotels, an alternative that this author's family chose.

The Roaring '20s were the last hurrah for most of the Jersey shore's grand hotels. Sprawling Victorian wooden hotels were still operational along the coast at the beginning of the 1920s although many of them had burned down or were updated beyond recognition. The largest concentration of luxury hotels existed on the Boardwalk at Atlantic City and people came from all over the nation, indeed from all over the world, to stay at them.

After the Great War, it was feared that Atlantic City was losing some of its wealthy clientele so hotel corporations schemed to lure them back. A New York Times article from November 1919, "Preserve for the Exclusive Rich at Atlantic City" details plans that would "cater to lavish spenders" and make Atlantic City "a rival of Monte Carlo in all but vice." Most well-heeled patrons of the luxury hotels still came by train, not by automobile. Some were even beginning to arrive by air.

The modern post-war high rise hotels boasted swift elevators, state-of-the art plumbing and fireproofing. Several large hotels were built in Atlantic City during the prosperous 1920s. At first, the traditional pompous décor with overstuffed sofas and potted palms continued, but innovative simpler and cleaner lines became more common by the close of the decade. Modernistic styles (coined "art deco" in the 1960s) with geometric lines debuted in Europe in 1925. The trend quickly spread to the United States with designs for everything from city skyscrapers to fashions and jewelry reflecting the new look.

Racial and religious bias kept a number of visitors from feeling comfortable at many of the grand hotels. In resort cities, there were Jewish run hotels specifically catering to clients who observed kosher dietary laws. In the early '20s, many of the big hotels frowned upon Jewish as well as Catholic guests. African Americans had few choices of places to stay and were not socially accepted at the hotels whose managers seemed to think of blacks only as hired help and as entertainers.

This chapter depicts a number of grand hotels as well as a variety of smaller places to stay during the 1920s at the New Jersey shore.

Room with a View. The Hotel Martin at Highlands commanded a great view of Sandy Hook and even Manhattan on a clear day. In this 1924 postcard, the Twin Lights on the hill can be seen in the background. A sign advertises the proverbial "Shore Dinner" a seafood meal that was offered at most every restaurant along the Jersey coast.

An "Art Deco" Architect's Work. Built in 1926 and designed by New York architect William Van Alen, the Renaissance Revival style Garfield-Grant Hotel at 275 Broadway was the largest year-round hotel in Long Branch at that time. Van Alen is best known for his design of New York's Chrysler Building (1930), an icon of what is now known as art deco. Named for two of the presidents who are associated with Long Branch history, The Garfield-Grant certainly cannot be compared with the beauty of Van Alen's celebrated skyscraper, but it is a good-looking, solid structure that survives today as an office building.

GARFIELD-GRANT HOTEL

A Hideaway at Waterwitch. Two fun-loving Roaring '20s couples pose for a casual photo at the once thriving hotel and bungalow compound at Waterwitch (Highlands). Conner's expanded in the '60s but by the mid-1980s, most of the bungalows were replaced with condominiums and the old hotel was demolished around 2000 to accommodate parking for a rapid ferry commuter service to New York

R-4—Molly Pitcher Hotel, Red Bank, N. J.

MONTEREY HOTEL, ASBURY PARK, N. J.

"The Molly." A splendid hotel on the Navesink River in Red Bank, The Molly Pitcher Inn that opened in 1929 is in business today and its exterior looks much the same. The Georgian Revival style is typical of the period revivals that were popular in the 1920s. Modernistic buildings were being constructed at the close of the decade, but many of the new buildings at the shore were more traditional designs.

A Classy Hotel. The New Monterey hotel located in North Asbury Park opened in 1912 and proved to be a popular destination for vacationers. The 364-room Spanish Revival hotel would set the pace for similar architecture in the area. In the Roaring '20s, The New Monterey was in its heyday and attracted stars of the Metropolitan Opera including Enrico Caruso and Amelita Galli-Curci as well as such notables as New York governor Al Smith and the Prince of Wales. The hotel was condemned in 1963 and demolished.

THE BERKELEY-CARTERET AND BOARDWALK, ASBURY PARK, N. J.
18

The "Gem" of the Jersey Shore. The red-brick Berkeley-Carteret hotel, designed by famous Beaux-Arts architect Warren Whitney and opened in 1925 is in operation today as The Berkeley Oceanfront Hotel. Although it's gone through several ownerships and changes, it still looks much the same as it did in this 1926 postcard. Situated across from the Paramount Theater and Convention Hall that opened in 1930, the grand hotel has been a haven for entertainers over the years. The New Monterey Hotel, seen in the background, had its view somewhat obstructed when the Berkeley-Carteret was built.

A Motel Predecessor. An advertisement for an Asbury Park "motor court" gives an idea of the new trend in the 1920s towards simple, inexpensive places where tourists with automobiles could park and stay.

128 BOARDWALK AND NEW MONTEREY, ASBURY PARK, N. J.

Riding the Ponies. A postcard mailed from Asbury Park in 1923 shows pony rides, always a delight for children. It cost 10 cents a ride to trek back and forth on the straight course parallel to the boardwalk. The New Monterey Hotel is in the background.

This stylish "art deco" ad for Asbury Park's Berkeley-Carteret appeared in the *Red Bank Register* in May, 1929.

Keep the Change. The humorous ditty on this 1924 postcard indicates that prices were dear at Asbury Park in the Roaring '20s. This type of postcard had a generic background and the resort name and a photo would be filled in by the printer.

A Stylish Hotel at Belmar. The Buena Vista on Second Avenue in Belmar that began as a much smaller establishment back in the 1880s had expanded to a large, fashionable hotel by the 1920s. By the mid-20th century, the Buena Vista was known as a popular kosher establishment that strictly observed Jewish dietary laws.

By the Beautiful Sea. The Atlantic Hotel on the oceanfront at Belmar between Fifteenth and Sixteenth Avenues went through many changes and additions by the time of this 1927 view. Tennis was popular in the Roaring '20s and here the hotel's court was near the front entrance. The Atlantic evolved from sections of the huge Machinery Hall that was transported to Belmar after the close of the 1876 Philadelphia Centennial. From the 1940s-60s, it was run by the McCann family and in 1972, it was destroyed by fire.

The Marconi "Hotel" (as it appeared from 1914 to the 1930s). "It's in Wall, but the Marconi Wireless Station was called Belmar because that's where the train station was. It was not actually a hotel but rather a dormitory for the wireless station workers who operated the station 24/7. One of the six 400-foot tall antenna masts can be seen behind the hotel. This building and others that Marconi constructed here in 1914 that served as part of a link in his world wide radio communications system are now in use by the InfoAge Group and serve as a Science-History Learning Center. They were used from 1941 to the 1990s as the Army's center for radar and other technology development as part of a greater Camp Evans." *Photo and caption courtesy of Ray Chase. Author's note: Also, the property was used as a headquarters for the KKK in the 1920s.*

HOTEL LA REINE, BRADLEY BEACH, N. J.

A Regal Hotel. One of the finest hotels in Bradley Beach, the LaReine is shown here at its oceanfront location in the 1920s. The hotel was actually rebuilt when it was moved in 1900 from its original location next to the Borough Hall and Fire Department on Main St. It featured a huge verandah and had a famous "Japanese Room" for parties. After being in business for 74 years, it burned to the ground in 1974.

THE ESSEX AND SUSSEX
from Private Bathing Beach
Spring Lake Beach, New Jersey

A Serene View. Spring Lake attracted a wealthy summer clientele in the '20s. The lovely Minna Pach, daughter of famous photographer Gustavus Pach, was photographed here c.1925 wearing a fashionable outfit. The beautiful St. Catharine's Church is visible in the background.

Spring Lake Classic. The Essex and Sussex Hotel at the attractive Monmouth County town of Spring Lake was a popular destination for sophisticated travelers in the Roaring '20s. The hotel is located between Essex Ave. and Sussex Ave. In this beautiful 1920s Albertype postcard, the guests are seen relaxing on the hotel's beach. The Essex and Sussex doubled for an Atlantic City hotel in the 1981 feature film *Ragtime* that was based on the novel by E.L. Doctorow. It stands today but has been converted into adult condominiums.

First Avenue, looking south, Manasquan, N. J.

The Engleside   Beach Haven, N. J.

Pitching a Tent. A fun-loving bunch of campers pose beside a tent and provisions at Long Beach Island in 1926. Perhaps they chose to stay out on the dunes and rough it. Or maybe a relative's beach house was too crowded and there was no other place to stay! *Collection of Margaret Thomas Buchholz.*

All in a Row. A c.1920 postcard of First Ave. looking south in Manasquan provides a good example of how the small summer bungalows appeared, many of them still in existence but updated. Brielle Rd. is the street on the right. Notice the automobiles; it looks like there's at least one for every home.

Rustic Cottages on LBI. On 77th St. in Harvey Cedars, c.1922, Jeanne, Bud and Louise Waite look ready to enjoy a sunny day playing at the beach. Model T's, can be seen on the packed gravel street. The summer homes, typical of many Long Beach Island cottages at that time, were simple wooden structures with no indoor plumbing. *Collection of Margaret Thomas Buchholz.*

A Grand Hotel on LBI. The Engleside at Beach Haven, a splendid Victorian with a round tower, was built by prosperous Quakers in 1876. Though considered sedate, the Engleside as seen in this 1920s Albertype postcard flourished during the 1920s and staged a big 50th anniversary bash in 1926. The hotel's tennis courts were popular in the Roaring '20s with many tournaments taking place. Professionals played there including Big Bill Tilden who won seventy American and international championships in his lifetime. The detailed story of the majestic Engleside that was demolished in 1943 can be found in *Eighteen Miles of History on Long Beach Island* by John Bailey Lloyd, Down the Shore Publishing, 1994.

Greetings from Atlantic City. The hotels of the Atlantic City skyline of the late 1920s can be seen inside the big letters of this Tichenor postcard.

HOTEL DENNIS -- WITH ITS "UNOBSTRUCTED OCEAN VIEW" — *Always open, on famed Atlantic City's ocean front*

"An Unobstructed Ocean View" – At Atlantic City, The Hotel Dennis was a popular destination in the '20s. It could be called the little hotel that grew and grew...and grew! Its origin goes back to "Professor" Dennis, a Burlington schoolmaster who built a two-room cottage in 1860 that expanded too quickly for Dennis who wanted a quiet retreat. He sold the oceanfront property in 1867 to Joseph H. Borton who made it into a larger boarding house with 250 rooms by 1892. In 1900, Walter Buzby bought the place and made it into a huge grand hotel. The Hotel Dennis has remained to the present day as part of Bally's Resort and Casino, although some sections of the old structure have been taken down.

MAIN LOUNGE, HOTEL DENNIS -- Magnificent Ocean Observatory — *on famed Atlantic City's ocean front*

The Dennis Interiors and Farm. (Above and opposite page) A series of postcards that was reprinted for many years depicts the elegant public rooms of the Hotel Dennis and shows the decor of the late '20s. The hotel dining room was "famed for its own farm foods." One card even shows that The Dennis had its own Jersey truck farm to provide delicious fresh produce for its guests.

A MARVEL SPOT – THE ST. DENIS ROOM IN HOTEL DENNIS – on famed Atlantic City's ocean front

THE HOTEL DENNIS LIBRARY HOLDS DISTINCTIVE CHARM – in Atlantic City, N. J.

HOTEL DENNIS DINING ROOM – FAMED FOR ITS OWN FARM FOODS – in Atlantic City, N. J.

DENNIS FARM DELICACIES DELIGHT HOTEL DENNIS DINERS – in Atlantic City, N. J.

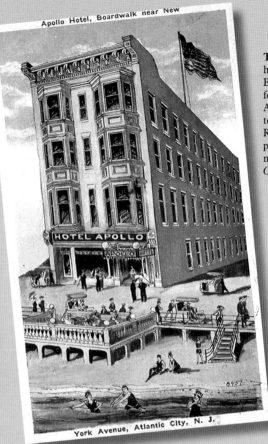

Apollo Hotel, Boardwalk near New

HOTEL APOLLO

York Avenue, Atlantic City, N. J.

The Apollo Hotel. One of the few small hotels that were on the Atlantic City Boardwalk, the Apollo became known for its art deco style. Situated next to the Apollo Theater, it housed many of the entertainers. The Apollo Hotel was previously Risley's Hotel and Restaurant. This 1920s postcard is an artist's view of the hotel minus the buildings that were on either side. *Collection of Allen "Boo" Pergament.*

The Breakers. Dating back to at least 1916, this elegant French chateau-style hotel on the Atlantic City Boardwalk was designed by south Jersey native Vivian Smith. The Breakers catered to a Jewish clientele and served outstanding homemade kosher food. The Breakers was imploded in 1974 along with the Hotel Rudolf, built in 1895, that was attached to it. There were also hotels on the avenues off the Boardwalk where Jews, who were not socially accepted at many of the Boardwalk establishments in the '20s, could enjoy their vacations. *Collection of Allen "Boo" Pergament.*

RITZ-CARLTON HOTEL

"Putting on the Ritz." Irving Berlin's 1929 tune about people getting all dressed up, refers to the phrase derived from the name of the stylish Ritz hotel chain. The gala opening of the Atlantic City Ritz Carlton at Iowa Ave. and Boardwalk on June 24, 1921, was one of the ritziest events imaginable! Notorious Atlantic City political figure, Enoch "Nucky" Johnson threw lavish parties here during the '20s-30s and gangland figures including Al Capone stayed at the Ritz. Though many of the grand hotels evolved from smaller wooden facilities that expanded, the Ritz with its 475 rooms was a child of the Roaring '20s and cost six million dollars to build. All sorts of glittering stage, musical, and movie stars stayed at the Ritz over the years, and its Merry-Go-Round Bar that opened after prohibition was a popular spot. The Ritz served as a home for troops during World War II, but then had financial difficulties and was converted into apartments in 1969.

AMBASSADOR HOTEL

The Ambassador and The Kingpins. In 1929, a three-day "gangster convention" was held at The Ambassador. It was an unprecedented meeting of high-level organized crime leaders including Al Capone, Lucky Luciano, Meyer Lansky, and Dutch Schultz. There may not have been a bar, but the mobsters no doubt enjoyed some of their illicit booze during their Ambassador stay as they puffed on big Havana cigars. This rare photo shows Capone walking on the Boardwalk with Nucky Johnson and an unknown man. Capone ended up as the "loser" at the get-together and left the resort with less power than he had before. In order to protect himself from hit men of his fellow kingpins, he took the train from Atlantic City to Philadelphia and turned himself in to police on a minor gun possession charge. He went to jail for a few months. It was Lucky Luciano who emerged from the Atlantic City convention with more importance than before.

"Beau Brummel of the Ritz." Enoch "Nucky" Johnson (c1883-1968), the son of a sheriff, began his political career in 1904. The Atlantic City political boss held a variety of offices in south Jersey. A colorful mobster known for wearing a carnation in his lapel, he was associated with bootlegging, illegal gambling, prostitution and other criminal activities. A personable man, he knew all the celebrities and was the resort's "official and unofficial host through the '20s and '30s" according to author William McMahon. In 1927, he became part of the mob group known as the "Big Seven" and he was an organizer of the 1929 Atlantic City "gangster conference." Convicted of tax evasion in the 1941, he married a former Ziegfeld showgirl shortly before he went to jail. Nucky returned to Atlantic City after serving four years, lived a quiet life, and died of natural causes at the age of eighty-five. *Collection of Allen "Boo" Pergament*

A Celebrated New Hotel. At the dawn of the Roaring '20s, a stylish hotel for the movers and shakers began. Constructed in two parts, the 200-room Ambassador at Boardwalk at Brighton Ave. (site of today's Tropicana) was built in 1919 and a 500-room section was added in 1921. A variety of famous people stayed at The Ambassador during the Roaring '20s including the notorious mobster Al Capone. According to author McMahon, The Ambassador was one of the few hotels opened without a bar in anticipation of the dry era to come. It finally got its bar, the famous "Horseshoe" in 1933. Paul Whiteman and his orchestra were regulars here and an unknown named Harry Crosby (later known as "Bing!") got his start.

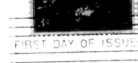

UNITED STATES POSTAGE

ATLANTIC CITY
JUN 9
9 AM
1947
N.J.

FIRST DAY OF ISSUE

Harry Houdini
American Escape Artist and Magician
St. Cecile Lodge No. 568, New York City

Sir Arthur Conan Doyle
Author of Sherlock Holmes, Physician
Phoenix Lodge No. 257, Portsmouth, England

Atlantic City, New Jersey, Circa 1922

The Magician and The Author. This first issue letter postmarked in Atlantic City from 1947 commemorates the Houdini-Doyle meeting in 1922 and gives information about their memberships in Masonic lodges. *Collection of Allen "Boo" Pergament.*

MIDWINTER SCENE SHOWING THE TRAYMORE HOTEL

The Famous Séance. Celebrities came to the New Jersey shore for a variety of reasons. In 1922, Harry Houdini (shown above), escape artist and debunker of spiritualism, and Sir Arthur Conan Doyle, creator of Sherlock Holmes and ardent believer in the paranormal, rendezvoused at Atlantic City. Doyle, on a lecture tour of the United States with his family, had lost a son in the World War and found comfort in spiritualism. He wanted to convince his friend Houdini by hosting a séance that the dead could be contacted. In a room at the Ambassador Hotel, Mrs. Doyle conducted the séance, "slipping into a trance" and conjuring up the spirit of Houdini's deceased mother. The illusionist missed his beloved mother terribly and wanted to believe. When Mrs. Doyle scribbled a long letter supposedly from his mother, Houdini kept silent but knew the truth. After Doyle and his family returned to England, Houdini revealed the details of the séance and explained that his mother spoke very little English and could not write in English. The message channeled by Mrs. Doyle was written in English.

A Colossal Hotel. The fourteen-story Hotel Traymore with its majestic twin tiled domes stood at Illinois Avenue and the Boardwalk. In the 1920s, it bustled all year round with activity as vacationers, honeymooners and conventioneers continuously occupied it. From its beginnings as wood frame cottage in 1879, it went through many changes. The building, as seen in this early 1920s postcard, was designed by William L. Price and completed in 1915. Finally, though not without a struggle, the grand old hotel gave in to travelers' preferences for motels and the rise of the casinos. In 1972, the Traymore was imploded (seen in the opening of 1980 Louis Malle motion picture "Atlantic City") and in a matter of seconds…the huge structure was gone forever.

The fourteen-story **Hotel Traymore**.

AT THE ENTRANCE OF THE MARLBOROUGH-BLENHEIM

A Concrete Hotel. Built in 1906 on the Boardwalk site of a former roller coaster, the Moorish-style Blenheim was constructed with reinforced concrete. It was one of the first fireproof hotels in Atlantic City. Thomas A. Edison, developer and owner of a cement-making process used for the construction, supervised the job. The Blenheim, depicted here in 1922, is also believed to be the first of the Atlantic City hotels to have a private bath for every room. The splendid hotel and its neighbor The Marlborough House (built in 1902) became the Marlborough-Blenheim. There were two enclosed bridges across Ohio Ave. that connected them, with the one near the Boardwalk for guests, and the one further back for the employees. Despite protests, the Blenheim was demolished in 1979, the year after the demise of The Marlborough House.

CRAIG HALL, SOUTH ILLINOIS AVENUE, ATLANTIC CITY, N. J.

Craig Hall. Not all the big Atlantic City hotels were along the boardwalk. Craig Hall on South Illinois Avenue (now Martin Luther King Blvd.) and Pacific Avenues is seen in this artist's rendition from its busy days in the late 1920s. Built by John Wyeth in the 1880s, the "skyscraper" then known as the Garden Hotel was sold to Robert Craighead and his brother James in 1910 at auction. The Craigheads were known as "ardent prohibitionists" and immediately removed all the bars. Prohibition didn't make any difference for this dry hotel. They are also credited with creating side street hotel rates, far lower than the Boardwalk prices. Craig Hall became Atlantic City's post office in 1935.

WEST WING OF ROOF PROMENADE, CRAIG HALL, ATLANTIC CITY, N. J.

EGYPTIAN ROOM SUN PARLOR ON ROOF PROMENADE,

CRAIG HALL, SOUTH ILLINOIS AVENUE, ATLANTIC CITY, N. J.

Up on the Roof. The west wing of the famous roof promenade of Craig Hall offered a view of the ocean although the building is not on the oceanfront. The distinctive twig arbor casts an intricate tracery of shadows. Hopefully, the patrons relaxing in rocking chairs didn't get a patterned tan! The guests in rocking chairs look content and prim, arguably not the way one might perceive "Roaring '20s" vacationers.

Egyptian Influence. With the discovery of King Tut's tomb and all its untouched treasures in 1922, the western world embraced Egyptian designs for decorating, clothing and jewelry. The Egyptian room sun parlor on the roof promenade of Atlantic City's Craig Hotel, c.1924, provides an excellent example of the craze. Notice the blue and orange motif including wallpaper, lamps on the mantle, picture, and window shade.

HOTEL CLARIDGE AT NIGHT, ATLANTIC CITY, N. J.—16

The Last Great Old Hotel. Its construction began at the end of the Roaring '20s, and the Claridge Hotel at the prestigious address of Boardwalk and Park Place opened on December 17, 1930. The eighteen-story Claridge featured the sleeker lines of the skyscrapers of the era and some people even note a certain resemblance to the Empire State Building. It survives today as the Claridge Casino Hotel. An early '30s linen era postcard illustrates the dazzling beauty of the fountain of light in front of the Claridge that was first lit up in 1929 during the Golden Jubilee of the Electric Light. It was renovated and restored including its colorful lighting in 2007. *Collection of Allen "Boo" Pergament.*

116:—Elephant Hotel, An Old Landmark on the Beach, Atlantic City, N. J.

Lucy on the Boardwalk. A replica of Lucy the Elephant and several beauties represented Atlantic City's neighbor Margate's attraction on a charming float in a Boardwalk parade c.1925. *Alfred M. Heston Collection, Atlantic City Free Public Library.*

Everybody Loves Lucy! Lucy the Elephant, an innovative piece of "zoomorphic architecture," was first built in 1881 by James V. Lafferty for the purpose of real estate promotion. Prospective land buyers could gaze out upon the desolate dunes and scrub pines of South Jersey from her 65 ft. high howdah. In the late 1880s, Lucy was sold to John and Sophie Gertzen who operated her as a tourist attraction and tavern with a hotel close by. In 1920, the bar closed because of prohibition but reopened after its repeal in 1933. This popular 1920s postcard depicts Lucy in her days as the "Elephant Hotel." Lucy is a survivor today despite years of deterioration and coming close to demolition in the 1960s. The 90-ton Lucy was moved from her original site in Margate to another location just two blocks away in 1970, thanks to a "Save Lucy" campaign and continues today as a museum and tourist attraction.

The Studio Cottage. Located on Pacific Ave. in Margate, this boarding house was the place where members of the author's family summered for several decades. This photo is from the early 1950s but it had not changed since the 1920s. The house that was owned by Harry Chambers, with its little decorative "prop" cottage, serves to represent many of the unpretentious places to stay that were close to big resorts. It had an ocean view from the high porch. No longer a place to stay, it is barely recognizable and a tall building blocks the view.

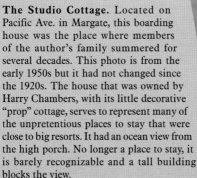

THE FLANDERS, BOARDWALK AT 11TH ST., OCEAN CITY, N.J.

The Flanders Early Days. The Flanders Hotel at Ocean City was not quite finished when its big opening dinner party was held there on July 28, 1923. The Spanish Mission Revival style hotel was designed by architect Vivian Smith who was born in Ocean City in 1886. Smith also designed Ocean City's 1929 music pier and several public buildings in South Jersey as well as the Breakers Hotel in Atlantic City (see page 36). This postcard of the Flanders, is dated 1925. An interesting sidelight… the printer mistakenly identified the hotel as being in Atlantic City (bottom), simply inked it over with marks, then printed the correct location at the top.

The Great Fire. A "before and after" postcard illustrates the destruction at Ocean City as a result of the 1927 blaze. The Flanders hotel is seen intact at the rear of the photos. According to a front page article of *The New York Times* (October 12, 1927), "The blaze started underneath the Boardwalk at the corner of Ninth Street, spread north and south a block each way and then under the bellows of a strong east wind of the ocean, drove westward for five avenues." The damage was estimated to be $4,000,000. New Jersey State troopers were brought in to guard the area from looters. ©*Ocean City Historical Museum, Inc.*

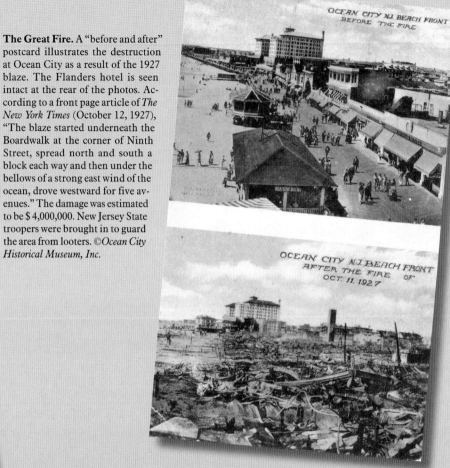

OCEAN CITY N.J. BEACH FRONT BEFORE THE FIRE

OCEAN CITY N.J. BEACH FRONT AFTER THE FIRE OF OCT. 11, 1927

THE FLANDERS, OCEAN CITY, N.J.—J. HOWARD SLOCUM, PRESIDENT, MANAGER.

Miraculous Survivor. The Flanders Hotel remained intact during the terrible fire of 1927 that destroyed much of the Ocean City boardwalk. This 1929 view can be compared to the 1925 postcard to see how the boardwalk was moved forward and some minor architectural changes were made to the building. Within a few years, a huge salt water swimming pool was built in the sandy area between the hotel and the boardwalk but has been replaced by rides and amusements today.

Ready to Serve. The waitresses at the Biscayne Hotel, 812 Ocean Avenue, (no longer there) in Ocean City were photographed in the dining room ready to serve the hotel patrons in the mid 1920s. The woman in the middle is most likely their supervisor. ©*Ocean City Historical Museum Inc.*

Modern Times. The Flanders Hotel is still in business today offering guest suites and banquet facilities. It is one of the few big 1920s Jersey shore hotels to survive. Emily's Ocean Room Café is named for a beautiful ghost, a lady in white who reportedly haunts The Flanders. The author stands outside the Flanders hotel at Ocean City on 11th Street in June 2008.

307. ARCADIA HOTEL, MAGNOLIA AND PACIFIC AVENUES, WILDWOOD-BY-THE-SEA, N. J.   82213

The Flanders's Fish. This 2008 photo shows an example of the '20s architectural ornamentation that is still on the well-preserved Ocean City hotel.

A Charming Place to Stay. Located at Magnolia and Pacific Avenues at Wildwood-By-The-Sea, The Arcadia Hotel was a cozy establishment that is depicted on this postcard from the 1920s. It's a far cry from the famous Wildwoods' doo wop motels of the 1950s that have recently been recognized as historic sites worthy of preservation.

CONGRESS HALL. CAPE MAY. N. J.

Cape May's Congress Hall. It began in 1816 as a simple boarding house owned by Thomas Hughes. He called it "The Big House" but locals thought it was too large and called it "Tommy's Folly." In 1828, Hughes was elected to Congress (which explains the name Congress Hall.) The hotel was destroyed in the big fire of 1878, but rebuilt within a year. Four US presidents stayed there – Grant, Pierce, Buchanan and Benjamin Harrison who made it his "Summer White House." It declined and was shut down from around 1905 until the 1920s when it flourished. Postmarked in 1927 and sent home to Philadelphia, the writer of this postcard said: "This is a very nice place and quiet for rest. It is cold at night and raining off and on." *Courtesy of Congress Hall, Cape May, NJ.*

The Staff of Congress Hall. The employees of the historic hotel on Beach Ave., Cape May, assembled c.1920 for this impressive panoramic portrait. Congress Hall is still in business today and is a popular place to stay or to hold special events. The current Brown Room was the location of Cape May's first post-Prohibition cocktail bar in 1934. *Courtesy of Congress Hall, Cape May, NJ.*

The main attraction at the Jersey shore in the Roaring '20s, or any decade, is the beach! The scenic waves and sounds of the pounding surf, the golden sand, the invigorating salt air, spectacular sunrises and sunsets…natural wonders that have beckoned vacationers to the New Jersey seashore since the late eighteenth century. Even before the first white tourists, Native Americans fished and clammed and appreciated the beauty of the untouched coast. Despite its development, New Jersey today has some of the best beaches in the country for swimming, surfing, fishing, and building sandcastles or simply relaxing!

An attraction often associated with the beach, particularly with the Roaring '20s, is the bathing beauty. Although beauty contests were conducted earlier, the first truly notable one was The Atlantic City Pageant in 1921, usually known as the "First Miss America Pageant." Along with the new morality and "liberation" came innovative styles in swimsuits as women dared to show the curves of their bodies. They either abandoned stockings while bathing or rolled them down. Men also dressed more liberally but tops were required for them at most resorts until the early 1940s. Men who refused to wear tops were called "beach nudists."

Not everyone looked like a Miss America or Tarzan. Photographs and postcards of the beach crowds in the '20s reveal all sorts of shapes, sizes, and ages. The media, much as it does today, promoted those perfect looking slender bodies that in reality were not the majority. Some people, especially the older adults, continued to wear the longer, loose traditional bathing costumes of their youth.

During the Roaring '20s, sunbathing became fashionable. In Victorian times such activity was taboo and suntans were associated with farm and outdoor workers. A tan became a status symbol as vacationers gained more mobility and those who could afford it, traveled to warm climates in winter. Although sun worshipers can be observed in the photos of the '20s Jersey shore, there were still many beach umbrellas and trendy oriental-style parasols. Beach tents were also used to provide some shade.

The New Jersey coast had plenty of shipwrecks over the years and the United States Lifesaving Service began in 1849. Along with increased numbers of people at the shore, there were more incidents of drowning. Bathers would hang onto ropes attached to poles in the water, but feared for their safety. "Constables of the Surf" were appointed to deal with emergencies at Atlantic City in 1855; and in the early 1870s, volunteer lifeguards called "bathing masters" began to patrol beaches along the coast. In the 1890s, Atlantic City organized a professional beach patrol, and by the 1920s, most resort towns along the coast employed lifeguards.

Photographs and postcards in this section include images of bathing beauties, beach patrols, and bathers (both the wealthy and the working class people although few photos exist of minorities). They all have one thing in common – the beach!

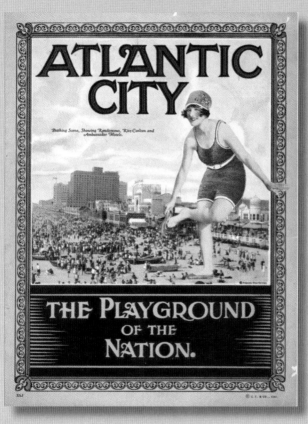

Beauty in a Red Bathing Suit. A Roaring '20s Atlantic City promotional booklet features a colossal bathing beauty on the cover. The publication touts "The Playground of the Nation" as having all-year-round appeal and calls its Boardwalk "The Promenade of the World."

There She Was! In 1921, a petite high school student named Margaret Gorman won the title of "Miss Washington DC" and a few months later became the "First Miss America" in what was then known as The Atlantic City Pageant. The September event was the brainchild of local business leaders in an attempt to extend Atlantic City's tourist season beyond the end of the summer. Gorman proudly posed in a flag cape and Statue of Liberty-style spiked crown after winning the Atlantic City contest. *Alfred M. Heston Collection, Atlantic City Free Public Library.*

America's Top Supermodels? "Inter-City beauties" line up on the Boardwalk during the first Miss America Pageant in 1921. The young women who represented various cities (not States at that time) are showing off the latest fashions and accessories including some fur wraps (complete with heads!). Their shoes and millinery are a fashion historian's delight. The winner and first "Miss America" Margaret Gorman is on the far left. *Alfred M. Heston Collection, Atlantic City Free Public Library.*

An Iconic Image. The poster designed for The Atlantic City Pageant of 1921 (first "Miss America" contest) was also made into a postcard. The same design was used for several successive 1920s pageants. *Collection of Allen "Boo" Pergament.*

Illustrated Boardwalk News, Sept. 18, 1922. *Collection of Allen "Boo" Pergament*

A Famous Blonde. Joan Blondell, "Miss Dallas," entered Atlantic City's 1926 "Miss America" pageant under the name "Rose-bud" Blondell. She placed fourth in the contest. The sultry blonde became a well known film star as seen on this early 1930s cigarette card.

A Royal Affair. The crowning of Miss America 1926 was an elaborate ceremony. In this popular photo, King Neptune places a crown on the winner, Norma Smallwood who was Miss Tulsa. The pretty Oklahoman had the distinction of being the first Native American (Cherokee) to become "Miss America." She is flanked by her court including another young woman of Native American descent (Spokane) named Alice Garry who appeared in the pageant as "Princess America." On the right is the Director-General of the pageant, Armand T. Nichols. WPG radio announcer Norman Brokenshire is ready to describe the event to the ever-increasing listeners at home. Miss America's "Golden Mermaid" trophy rests on the bottom step. *Alfred M. Heston Collection, Atlantic City Free Public Library.*

Atlantic City Inter City Beauties 1925. The winner was Fay Lanpier, "Miss California," the first Miss America to represent a state.
Library of Congress.

Look Inside! This Atlantic City card with bathing beauties inside the letters is postmarked 1928.

A Mermaid Rides By. A live mermaid graces the Dennis Hotel's float that is in a typical Atlantic City Boardwalk parade lineup of displays, c.1925, probably during the Miss America pageant.
Alfred M. Heston Collection, Atlantic City Free Public Library.

Presenting Miss Long Branch. Nineteen-year old Elene Hicks of Long Branch won a local beauty contest during the Long Branch Carnival that celebrated the paving of Ocean Ave. in August 1923. She went on to The Atlantic City Pageant as one of the Inter-city beauties (the women represented cities in the early Miss America competitions, not States). Despite her down-to-earth charm, Elene didn't win and the crown went to Mary Campbell of Columbus, Ohio, who won the title in both 1922 and 1923. There was no talent competition yet, but Elene, an accomplished pianist, would have done well. She married and had one daughter who was named for her. Sadly, Elene, the first and only Miss Long Branch, died of breast cancer in 1940 at the age of thirty-eight. *Courtesy of Elene Dwyer.*

An ad from a 1921 *Theatre* magazine.

The Latest Swimwear. Three of the 1923 "Miss Long Branch" contestants are showing off their form-fitting Annette Kellerman bathing suits. Elene Hicks (middle) was the contest winner. Australian-born Kellerman, a champion swimmer and star of vaudeville and silent films capitalized on her fame with a line of beach wear. Previously, suits were knee length, loose garments that hid the curves of the body and were difficult to swim in. By the close of the 1920s, the one piece tank suit for women was commonly accepted. *Courtesy of Elene Dwyer.*

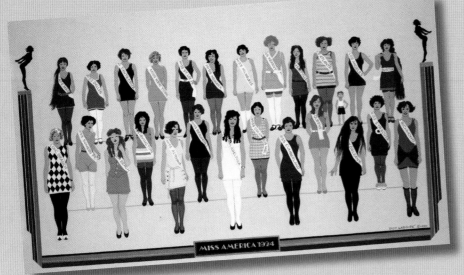

"**Miss America 1924.**" Renowned Jersey shore artist, Dick LaBonté researched the bathing costumes worn by these Atlantic City Pageant contestants for his 1990 acrylic on panel painting. He chose twenty-five of the eighty-three entrants who represented various cities. Miss Long Branch, Elene Hicks, is on the far left in the first row. (She was in the 1923 pageant; it was not unusual for young women to enter more than once.) The winner was Miss Philadelphia, Ruth Malcolmson. ©1990 Courtesy of La Bonté Prints, Inc.

A Trendsetting Star. Annette Kellerman's bathing suits were all the rage at the Jersey Shore in the 1920s. The daring Kellerman was even arrested at Revere Beach, Massachusetts, in the early years of the century because of her "skimpy" bathing costume. Swimmer Gertrude Ederle (see p. 95), first woman to swim the English Channel (1926) claimed that she invented the form-fitting bathing suit, but "didn't have the sense to patent it."

Ephemeral Beach Art. A sand artist stands in front of his beach "gallery" near the steel pier hoping that an appreciative tourist will give him a donation. Elaborate sand sculptures were an attraction at the Atlantic City beach from the 1890s until 1944 when the hurricane washed them out and the city decided to prohibit them. In this postcard view, the work in the middle depicts the 1921 Inter-City (original Miss America) contest and the painting on the right is in tribute to Lindbergh's famous 1927 solo flight. Asbury Park and several other resorts also had talented sand artists during this period.

LIFE GUARDS, BOARDWALK, ATLANTIC CITY, N. J.

AC's Beach Patrol on Parade. During the Atlantic City Pageant (first "Miss America" contest) of 1921, a good-looking group of life guards from the Atlantic City Beach Patrol are marching down the Boardwalk with their float. The distinctive red sign of the "F.W. Woolworth Co. 5 and 10 Cent Store" can be seen in the background.

African Americans of "The Nation's Playground." The George Walls Bath House (upper left corner) is listed at 2617 Boardwalk (Texas Ave.) in a 1922 Atlantic City directory. It was owned by an African American businessman. These attractive African American women representing Walls Bath House are posing with two members of the Atlantic City beach patrol that was integrated. Ruth Walls is the first young woman on the right. The man who can be seen standing near the center in back of the women may be her father, the bath house owner. The group appears ready to march in the parade that was part of the Miss America pageant festivities. In the 1920s, there was widespread informal segregation and Boardwalk hotel owners complained when African Americans used beaches where they could be seen by their guests. Although not posted, it was clear that people of color were "socially restricted." Some did go to other beaches in the '20s, but the beach at Missouri Ave. was considered the only one acceptable for black visitors who were bused there in the 1930s. The local African Americans followed them and, in the 1950s, nicknamed it "Chicken Bone Beach." It was recognized as a local historical land site by the Atlantic City Council in 1997. *Alfred M. Heston Collection, Atlantic City Free Pubic Library.*

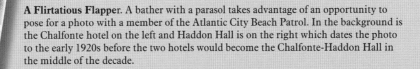

A Flirtatious Flapper. A bather with a parasol takes advantage of an opportunity to pose for a photo with a member of the Atlantic City Beach Patrol. In the background is the Chalfonte hotel on the left and Haddon Hall is on the right which dates the photo to the early 1920s before the two hotels would become the Chalfonte-Haddon Hall in the middle of the decade.

LIFE GUARD EXPLAINING LENGTH OF BATHING SUITS TO BE WORN, ATLANTIC CITY, N. J.

Restrictions. Some members of the Atlantic City Beach Patrol are telling these young women about the rules for the length of bathing suits. *Collection of Allen "Boo" Pergament.*

Having a Wonderful Time! These unidentified young people at an Atlantic City area beach are wearing great looking bathing fashions typical of the Roaring '20s. A gentle-looking dog is keeping them company. *Vicki Gold Levi Collection.*

BATHING, HIGHLAND BEACH, N. J.

Highland Beach. Located near the Highlands Bridge, a popular bathing pavilion on the Shrewsbury River is depicted on a c.1920 postcard. It was not in Highlands; it was a part of Sandy Hook, Middletown Township. The resort, that was on both the river and ocean sides of Ocean Ave, no longer exists. It was a popular spot for day trippers from Newark and New York because it was easy to reach, but the traffic jams to get there could be terrible.

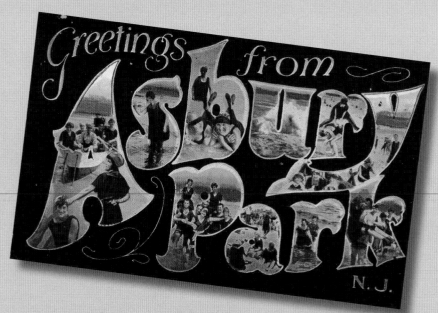

Greetings from Asbury Park N.J.

Greetings from Asbury Park. No, this is not the card used for Bruce Springsteen's legendary 1973 *Greetings from Asbury Park* album. It is an earlier, 1920s version of a big letter card but both cards are Tichenor views. Peek inside the letters to see some bathing beauties and people having fun at the beach.

LIFE GUARD, ASBURY PARK, N.J.

Life Savers. At the Asbury Park beach in the 1920s, a beefy group of life guards pose for a photographer as onlookers observe from the boardwalk. The guard in the center of the front row appears to be older and was most likely in charge.

Beach and Boardwalk, Ocean Grove, N. J.

Wholesome Ocean Grove. A 1921 postcard shows the beach at this clean and healthy family resort. Ocean Grove was founded in 1869 by the Methodist Camp Meeting Association. The site of Anti-Saloon League and Women's Christian Temperance Union meetings over the years, Ocean Grove welcomed prohibition. Besides its famous "tent city," the resort had charming hotels and rental cottages available for the 1920s vacationers. The social life revolved around the programs at the great Auditorium which had not only religious services but also concerts and movies. Some things haven't changed much in the dry town that retains its Victorian architecture and is a popular tourist spot today.

BOARDWALK AND BEACH FROM LA REINE HOTEL, BRADLEY BEACH, N. J.

The Crowd at Bradley Beach. This 1920s postcard shows the Monmouth County resort town's popular boardwalk and beach as viewed from the LaReine Hotel. It appears that some of these strollers might have been added into the picture. Two women are wearing bathing suits which would not have been allowed on the boardwalk at that time. Can you spot them? A miniature golf course is visible on the ocean side and the man in the left hand corner appears to be flying a kite.

Generic Bathing Beauties. (Below and opposite page) Postcard companies often used stock photos of models in bathing costumes and then added the names of "Atlantic City," "Asbury Park," or other resorts to them, or simply did not specify a location. The cards reflect the popular styles worn by young women during the Roaring '20s. Some of them were considered to be quite risqué, especially the well-endowed model on the Seaside Heights card.

Some of our Girls, Atlantic City, N. J.

JUST MY STYLE.

Belmar Beauties. Oriental style parasols were all the rage in the Roaring '20s. On the far left is Mildred Henning (Mildred Desmond Day), who loaned this photo to the author in the 1990s. Mildred was a lovely and well-known Belmarian who was active in community affairs.

Being well entertained
in
Seaside Heights

So don't
expect me back
for a while

A Pebble on the Beach,

Fishing for Lobsters.

145A. ATLANTIC CITY, N. J. MERELY A MATTER OF FORM.

A Sunny Day at Long Branch. In this 1923 photo, vacationers are basking in the sun and enjoying the surf near the old Long Branch pier. The 48-star flag is lowered, due to the death of President Warren G. Harding in August of 1923.

"It Floats." Another type of generic postcard was the unflattering, humorous kind. On this card postmarked from Asbury Park in 1922, the plump old fashioned-looking bather is a far cry from the '20s ideal of the slim flapper.

A Local Family at the Beach. The Eigenrauch family posed for some informal portraits at Long Branch c.1922. The Long Branch Pier is in the background. A poultryman from nearby Middletown, NJ, Henry Eigenrauch Sr. and his wife, Jessie, regularly enjoyed the beach with their children as many local people did during the Roaring '20s. Their sons who are pictured here are Henry, Jr. (rear) and in the front (left to right) are Herbert William, Christian, and Robert. *Courtesy of Jane Eigenrauch.*

Long Branch Beach Crowd. This view of the Long Branch beach is looking south, in the area of today's Pier Village and McLoone's Pier House restaurant, probably taken in 1923 on the same day as the previous photo. Notice how far back the beach is and the small jetties placed to help with erosion all along the stretch of beach.

"The Twenties." The summer crowd at the Bay Head beach in the Roaring '20s is delightfully captured by artist Dick LaBonté in his 1992 acrylic on canvas painting. The house on the left was named "Ashanti" and the one on the right was named "Peek-A-Boo Cottage." Take the time to look at each person and don't miss the couple under the boardwalk! ©1992 Courtesy of LaBonté Prints, Inc.

At "Point" Beach. Casual visitors to the Point Pleasant Beach in the Roaring '20s are sitting on the edge of the boardwalk that has no railings. The four flappers on the right side appear to be having a fun-filled day at the popular beach.

BOARDWALK ALONG THE BEACH, POINT PLEASANT BEACH, N. J.

BATHING BEACH, MANASQUAN, N. J.

Men at Leisure. A group of young men look like they are having fun at the Manasquan bathing beach in this 1920s postcard. Notice that they are all wearing muscle shirts as men were not allowed to go topless on New Jersey beaches until the early 1940s.

Fur at the Beach. Fur was fashionable throughout the Roaring '20s, and worn not only to keep warm in winter but even at the beach in summer! These two photos of unidentified flappers were taken at the Ocean City Beach. ©*Ocean City Historical Museum, Inc.*

A Sad Sight. These Jersey shore tourists were photographed with a large beached whale that had died, the cause probably unknown. Written on the photo is: "Whale Ashore, May 3, 1929, 62 feet, 58 tons." ©*Ocean City Historical Museum Inc.*

SCENE ON BEACH DURING BATHING HOURS, CAPE MAY, N. J.

Parking for the Beach. It appears that many of the people on this beach at Cape May drove there, judging from all those parked cars. An officer is making sure some bathers get safely across the street and a man, front and center, is waving enthusiastically to the photographer.

OCEAN CITY IS JUST ONE GIRL AFTER ANOTHER

Ocean City Beauties. A "chorus line" of athletic-looking young women on the Ocean City beach show off for the photographer in a late 1920s photo by The Senior Studio. The original caption reads: "Ocean City is just one girl after another." *From "Shore Chronicles: Diaries and Travelers Tales from the Jersey Shore." Edited by Margaret Thomas Buchholz ©1999. By permission of Down the Shore Publishing.*

Funchase Bathing. Wildwood's bathing beach near the old Funchase Pier is depicted on this 1920s postcard. The spacious beach had a row of tent-like cabanas for those who were careful not to get too much sun. The Funchase Pier had a popular roller skating rink. It later became Hunt's Pier that is no longer in operation.

Cape May Locals. Not everyone had to drive a distance to get to the beach. These two Cape May beach photos are from an early 1920s photo album belonging to the Reeves family who lived on a farm at Cold Spring (Cape May).

9 BATHING BEACH NEAR FUNCHASE PIER WILDWOOD, N. J.

Attack of the Giant Bather! Exaggerated "tall tale" postcards were all the rage. This smiling young woman is added (and without computer imaging!) into the surf at Wildwood on a card postmarked in 1922.

BATHING SCENE, FROM OCEAN PIER, WILDWOOD, N. J.

"Along the Jersey Coast." In describing this painting that resembles Spring Lake but represents any charming seaside resort, well-known Jersey shore artist Dick LaBonté says: "I chose it for an imaginary, carefree scene of the '20s in which an endless, empty boardwalk stretches to the vanishing point." The 1987 work by LaBonté is acrylic on panel. ©1987 *Courtesy of LaBonté Prints, Inc.*

61

Think of the Jersey shore boardwalks in the summertime and images of cotton candy, carousels, ice cream cones, and games of chance come to mind. The good old fashioned amusements and traditions that began in the late 1800s are still with us. But the actual locations for these pastimes and treats have dwindled down as home video games, DVDs, freezer popsicles, and microwave popcorn have replaced them.

In the 1920s, people were discovering the world of home entertainment with the advent of radio broadcasts. First it was recordings on the Victrola, and now, for the first time in history, they could listen to live band music, opera stars, comedy teams, sporting events, and concerts right in their own home. Live shows flourished at the Jersey shore with vaudeville and Broadway tryouts, but the movies became increasingly well-attended. The silent photoplays were popular, but with the advent of the talkies in the late '20s, more movie theaters popped up everywhere. Some of the big piers offered movies but thrilling live acts such as the High Diving Horse rivaled other forms of boardwalk entertainment and continued to do so for decades. There are some things you simply must experience in person.

Most amusements, especially at the smaller beach towns, were seasonal but at Atlantic City and other larger resorts, hotels were open all year and there were cold weather activities. Walking the boards, riding in rolling chairs bundled up in blankets, horseback riding on the beach, indoor spas and pools, and of course the shows and movies, were just some of the things to do in the off season.

In the Roaring '20s, the public was enthralled by all the latest innovations in technology and boardwalk displays provided hours of free entertainment, much to the delight of the industries. The 20's tourist delighted in seeing exhibits of the latest automobiles, home appliances, processed foods, cosmetics, and new fabrics for clothing.

The illustrations in this chapter cover a wide variety of things that were enjoyed by Jersey shore vacationers of the 1920s. From the simple amusements at the Long Branch pier, to the Broadway tryouts at Atlantic City or a Saturday movie matinee at Bay Head, to the taste of a delicious shore dinner almost anywhere along the coast…there was never a lack of things to do at the Jersey shore, even on a rainy day.

Have a Drink! A charming young server sells fresh squeezed lemon juice and Hires Root Beer for 10 cents a cup at the Long Branch pier in 1923. These acceptable drinks during those prohibition years provided refreshing treats in the heat of the summer.

Innocent Family Fun. The simple Long Branch recreation pier of the 1920s provided a fun-filled haven for families. A 1923 ad for the pier listed "Refined Amusements, Dancing, Riding Devices and Refined Games." D.J. Maher was the owner. This pier later became known as "the fishing pier." Eventually, it was the site of "The Haunted Mansion" and other amusements that burned down in 1987. Today the modern Pier Village complex with condominiums, restaurants and shops occupies the same area where the old pier and amusements were.

Up, Up and Away! The airplane swing on the Long Branch pier had a tower about 40 feet high. It had been there since 1913 and made a big hit with the kids in the '20s when the rapidly growing aviation industry was making headlines. The small planes on the ride were attached to wires that would swing out as the top of the tower rapidly rotated.

Try Your Luck! This photograph is of a "refined" adult game of chance at the Long Branch pier in the early 1920s, although it's not possible to see exactly what they were playing. Gambling for cash was not allowed, but prizes that were awarded are clearly visible including typical 1920s style lamps, china, figurines and clocks.

Test Your Skill! Step right up and see if you can win a prize! At one of the amusement booths on the Long Branch pier in the early 1920s, a crowd gathers to play a game. Participants are trying to win some china plates or a tea set, inexpensive in their day but now treasured collectibles.

A Stunning Entertainment Complex. At the close of the Roaring '20s, the construction of Asbury Park's Paramount Theater and Convention Hall designed by Whitney Warren of the famed New York firm of Warren and Wetmore, caused a stir of excitement. Viewed here from the water, the entertainment venues that are joined by a closed arcade opened in 1930 and are still thriving today with ongoing restoration taking place. The Berkeley-Carteret Hotel is on the left.

A Celebration. These autos are lined up at the entrance to the Long Branch pier in 1923 preparing for the grand "Jubilee and Mardi Gras" to celebrate the paving of Ocean Avenue. The event included a parade, beauty contest, band concerts, a masked carnival and political speeches.

Fanciful Decorations. The outside of the Boardwalk arcade connecting Asbury Park's Paramount Theater and Convention Hall has undergone restoration as seen in this 2008 photo. Mythical fish, seahorses, and a ship are among the architectural details.

OCEAN AVENUE DURING BABY PARADE, ASBURY PARK, N. J.

Beautiful Babies. The granddaddy of baby parades at the Jersey shore, Asbury Park's event was started in 1890 by James A. Bradley and became the annual Children's Carnival and Baby Parade. The popular summer festival was put on hold during the First World War, but started up again in the 1920s. Although Asbury Park was the first, many other shore towns also had annual baby parades.

Princess Flora. Miss Evelyne Kane, of 604 Third Ave., Asbury Park, was a princess and attendant to "Queen Titania" at the annual Asbury Park Baby Parade and Carnival in August, 1924. The rhinestone pendant she's wearing is a lovely example of a popular jewelry style of the Roaring '20s.

Jenkinson's Pavilion and Beach from Fishing Pier, Point Pleasant Beach, N. J.

A Pleasant Place. Jenkinson's Pavilion and Beach located at Point Pleasant Beach first opened in 1928. Businessman Charles Jenkinson owned soda fountains at Asbury Park and Ocean Grove in the early 1900s, but became tired of restrictions placed on him by his landlords. In 1926 he bought property in Point Pleasant Beach and soon converted its quiet boardwalk into a lively site with a candy shop and soda fountain at his pavilion, and a swimming pool and novelty store across from it. A year later he added a dance hall and a miniature golf course. Jenkinson's has expanded over the years but remains one of the Jersey shore's most popular family destinations.

365:—Aeroplane View of Steel Pier, Atlantic City, N. J.

"Showplace of the Nation." Making its debut in 1898, the Atlantic City Steel Pier offered classical concerts, brass bands, opera singers, variety acts, and even a seal tank. In July 1924, a raging fire caused extensive damage to the Steel Pier. The following summer it was sold to "Atlantic City's Barnum" Frank P. Gravatt and on June 12, 1926, a grand opening celebrated the newly managed and renovated pier that included a studio for radio station WPG. The Marine Ballroom hosted dance bands where patrons could show off their Foxtrot and Charleston. This is an early 20th century "aeroplane" view postcard of the Steel Pier.

A Flapper and her Dog. At Point Pleasant Beach, Edna Biddle and "Teddy" enjoy a walk on the boards, c.1924.

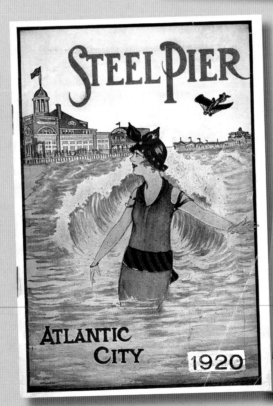

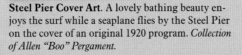

Steel Pier Cover Art. A lovely bathing beauty enjoys the surf while a seaplane flies by the Steel Pier on the cover of an original 1920 program. *Collection of Allen "Boo" Pergament.*

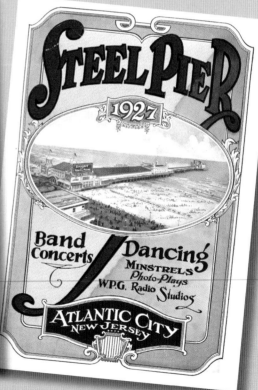

A vintage 1927 Steel Pier Program gives a bird's eye view of the pier and contains programs for concerts by Sousa and his Band.

These radio towers and logo for WPG appeared on the cover of a booklet about the station. This was a municipally-owned station that first aired in January 1925 and was located at the end of the Steel Pier. The second station in Atlantic City, it was preceded by WHAR at the old Seaside Hotel. *Collection of Allen "Boo" Pergament.*

The Hottest New Automobiles! Also in 1926, the Steel Pier was expanded to accommodate the General Motors Exhibit, a popular attraction due to the growing automobile industry in the 1920s and America's love affair with cars. These three postcards are examples of promotional material for the latest Pontiacs that were being previewed at the Steel Pier General Motors exhibit in the late '20s. A curvy model in a red swimsuit accentuates the beauty of the latest Pontiac 2-door sedan that's parked on the beach to attract attention.

156 VIEW OF SPACIOUS MARINE BALLROOM—OCEAN END ATLANTIC CITY STEEL PIER, ATLANTIC CITY, N. J.

374-29

A Jam-Packed Ballroom. In the late '20s and early '30s, postcards like this one showed how many people the spacious Marine Ballroom at the ocean end of the Steel Pier could hold. The capacity was approximately 4,000! Did they have any fire laws? Various celebrity bands played here including Paul Whiteman's band. The well-dressed group seen here with banjo and sax is not identified, but surely someone will recognize the older woman in the center who is wearing a fashionable hat and pearls.

158 SOUSA AT STEEL PIER, ATLANTIC CITY, N. J.

GENERAL MOTORS EXHIBIT

SOUSA AND HIS BAND

S461-29

Hail the Arrival of Sousa. "The March King" Sousa and his band arrive at the Steel Pier in a coach fit for royalty (but without horses!) The seated woman in the red dress is likely a singer. A crowd greets them along with pier owner and impresario Frank P. Gravatt (third from left in front right) and some officials. Signs for the General Motors Exhibit, Diving Horses, Human Cannonball, and on the right a film, "Pleasure Crazed" (that gives the clue to the year of this image, 1929) and more are all visible in this postcard.

127 CROWDED STANDS WITNESS HORSE DIVE—STEEL PIER, ATLANTIC CITY, N. J.

S464-29

A Class Act. The High Diving Horse, the Steel Pier's most memorable attraction of them all, brought in huge crowds. This c.1929 postcard depicts the diving horse and rider emerging from the pool. The backside of the famous Texaco sign on the pier can be seen.

Two Beauties on a Horse. High Diving Horse equestriennes Lorena Carver (holding the reins), daughter of Wild West showman Doc Carver (Buffalo Bill's original partner) who originated the act, and her sister-in-law Sonora Webster Carver look terrific sitting on one of the diving horses on the beach by the Steel Pier. The performing quarter horses were well treated though animal welfare groups kept a close eye on them. Sonora lost her sight in 1931 after hitting the water with her eyes open, but she continued the act for eleven years not letting the public know of her plight. Sonora married Al Carver, Doc's son. A 1991 Walt Disney movie, *When Wild Hearts Can't Be Broken,* was loosely based on her life story. Sonora lived well into her nineties. *Alfred M. Heston Collection, Atlantic City Free Public Library.*

Taking the Plunge. "Red Lips," one of high diving horses, and rider Sonora Webster Carver were captured in motion by photographer Kelso Taylor on the way down from the 40-foot high tower. This iconic image is from the early 1930s, but the act originated in the early 20th century, toured the country and made a big splash when it opened at the Steel Pier in 1929. Audiences loved it and the stunt continued there for decades with several different horses and riders. One of them, Arnette Webster French (Sonora's sister), said "the horse was in charge." *Alfred M. Heston Collection, Atlantic City Free Public Library.*

A Stunning Reflection. In 1929, High Diving Horse "John the Baptist" and rider "Maria" stand by the pool that they regularly jumped into from a high tower. The men next to them are "March King" John Philip Sousa and Frank P. Gravatt who owned the pier. The stands were usually packed to capacity but this photo may have been taken after the act as some of the spectators had already left. *Alfred M. Heston Collection, Atlantic City Free Public Library.*

414:—Steeplechase Pier, Atlantic City, N. J.

The Funny Pier. In 1902, George C. Tilyou, the celebrated Coney Island amusement operator, took over a pier constructed in 1899 at the foot of Pennsylvania Ave. Known as the Auditorium Pier, it got off to a rocky start after protests from nearby hotels and local officials. Although Tilyou booked such favorites as Sousa's band and the Floradora Sextet, the place simply wasn't doing well. Then in 1904 when Tilyou decided to refurbish the pier as a Coney Island style amusement place…success! He renamed it the Steeplechase and it made a hit with crowds who loved "the funniest place on earth."

The undated postcard above appears to be from around 1919-1920 and the entrance is a big toothy open clown mouth.

52. STEEPLECHASE PIER, ATLANTIC CITY, N. J.

Funny Face. Postmarked 1927, the card below shows the "Tillie" face with Tilyou's name and sign identifying the pier as "The Funny Place" at the entrance and whimsical decorations of toy soldiers, a quaint village with windmills and charming animals. People even rented clown costumes to wear while visiting the pier. It was great fun while it lasted but in on February 14, 1932, the pier was totally destroyed by fire. It was rebuilt and in operation into the 1970s, but was never quite the same.

The "Pickle" Pier. Opened in 1898 by pickle tycoon Henry J. Heinz of Pittsburgh, this pier at Massachusetts Ave. was originally known as The Iron Pier. Heinz ran organ concerts and sing-a-longs but the crowds wanted something new and business dropped off. When Heinz began to give out free samples of his "57" varieties of pickles and other products and even "pickle pins" to pier visitors, it became very popular. This print ad depicts the pier in 1924 and shows the famous "57" sign. Some of the foods used were grown and canned in New Jersey. The hurricane of 1944 destroyed the pier and the site was returned to the city. The Heinz Company thrives today as a global operation and the company history is preserved at The Senator John Heinz Regional History Center in Pittsburgh.

Model Kitchen, Crane National Exhibit, Boardwalk, Atlantic City, N. J.

GARDENS IN FRONT OF B. F. KEITH'S THEATRE, ATLANTIC CITY, N. J.

Garden by the Sea. The Garden Pier (seen here on a postcard c.1920) east of New Jersey Ave., lived up to its name with a variety of flowering shrubs. Built in 1913, it featured the impressive B.F. Keith vaudeville theater at its ocean end where big name stars appeared. Rudy Vallee debuted in "George White's Scandals" and Houdini performed his amazing escape acts. The pier eventually declined and was taken over by the City in the 1940s. The theater was demolished a few years after the 1944 hurricane, rebuilt and the two side structures were restored. It's now the home of the Atlantic City Historical Museum and The Cultural and Arts Museum.

Crane's Model Kitchen. Along the Atlantic City Boardwalk, tourists could visit free exhibits of the latest products, technological innovations and fashionable new styles from a number of diverse companies. The Crane National Exhibit of plumbing supplies proved to be popular in the 1920s when many new homes were being built and old ones updated. This pristine "model kitchen" from the Crane exhibit may look dull today, but to the homeowner or builder of the 1920s, it was exciting!

Keyboarding for a Giant? The huge Underwood typewriter, displayed in Atlantic City for 22 years, weighed 14 tons and was 21 feet wide by 18 feet high. It really worked as evidenced by the 9 ft. wide by 12 ½ ft. high letter seen on this 1920s postcard. The machine was far cry from today's computers, but school children of that era were awestruck by this marvel. First made in 1915 by the Underwood Corporation for the Panama-Pacific Exposition in San Francisco, it went to Atlantic City the following year where it remained for twenty-two years, first on the Garden Pier and later in a Convention Hall store on the boardwalk. It went to the 1939 New York World's Fair, and was eventually turned into scrap metal during World War II.

GIANT UNDERWOOD TYPEWRITER, UNDERWOOD GARDEN PIER EXHIBIT, ATLANTIC CITY, N. J.

405:—Young's Million Dollar Pier, Atlantic City, N. J.

Spectacular Advertisements. In the 1920s, boardwalks became not only a place to stroll or to ride in a rolling chair; they were venues for promoting products. Some were simple billboards; others were extravagant electric signs. The R.C. Maxwell Company's Electric Sign Manufacturing Company in Atlantic City created amazing displays including the colossal ad on the Steel Pier for Chesterfield cigarettes that contained over 27,000 light bulbs, "the largest sign of its kind in the world." Mr. Maxwell meticulously documented his company's work with outstanding photographs that show the surroundings including buildings and people, giving wonderful details about the era. The entire R.C. Maxwell collection that belongs to the Rare Books, Manuscripts and Special Collections Library of Duke University provides a visual treasure trove of information about Atlantic City, Asbury Park and other locations as well as familiarity with the popular products of the 1920s. Four of the Atlantic City photographs are presented here. *With thanks to Allen "Boo" Pergament and by permission of Duke University Library.*

New York Ave. and Boardwalk. R.C. Maxwell and Company signs advertise Maxwell House Coffee and Van Raalte Silk Stockings, Underwear, and Gloves in this photograph from June 11, 1922. Nixon's Apollo Theater and Apollo Hotel as well as the Alamac Hotel are seen here and the Dobkin Studio (photography) is to the left of the Apollo Hotel. *RC Maxwell Collection, Duke University Rare Book, Manuscript, and Special Collections Library, #MO343.*

The Captain's Million Dollar Showplace.
Eccentric showman Captain John Lake Young's Million Dollar Pier at Arkansas Ave. rocked with entertainment. First opened in 1906, it was the "home of the Cakewalk" and had a Hippodrome where great stars performed. Young's personal villa, #1 Atlantic Ocean, with much statuary and gaudy ornamentation was at the end of the pier. In the Roaring '20s dance bands would play and the Million Dollar Pier was the site of the longest dance marathon ever held at Atlantic City in 1932.

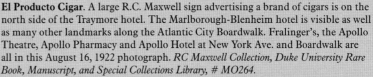

El Producto Cigar. A large R.C. Maxwell sign advertising a brand of cigars is on the north side of the Traymore hotel. The Marlborough-Blenheim hotel is visible as well as many other landmarks along the Atlantic City Boardwalk. Fralinger's, the Apollo Theatre, Apollo Pharmacy and Apollo Hotel at New York Ave. and Boardwalk are all in this August 16, 1922 photograph. *RC Maxwell Collection, Duke University Rare Book, Manuscript, and Special Collections Library, # MO264.*

Boardwalk Near The Garden Pier. The date of this Atlantic City photo is September 8, 1921. Many fascinating details about the shops and the crowd can be observed. An R.C. Maxwell sign for Piedmont Cigarettes is featured, and the St. Charles Hotel can be seen in the background. A "Comfort Station" (restrooms) for strollers and bathers is visible near the center on the beach, one of four that were located along the length of the Boardwalk. *RC Maxwell Collection, Duke University Rare Book, Manuscript, and Special Collections Library, #MO274.*

Boardwalk in Winter. A February 22, 1923, photograph documents winter fashions worn on the Atlantic City Boardwalk. Everyone appears well dressed and many of the women are wearing fur-trimmed coats. An R.C. Maxwell sign for Velvet Tobacco is on the Steeplechase Pier and a sign for the Gillette Safety Razor is close by. The Steel Pier can be seen just a little to the north and on the left is the Haddon Hall hotel. *RC Maxwell Collection, Duke University Rare Book, Manuscript, and Special Collections Library, #MO411.*

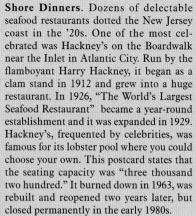

Shore Dinners. Dozens of delectable seafood restaurants dotted the New Jersey coast in the '20s. One of the most celebrated was Hackney's on the Boardwalk near the Inlet in Atlantic City. Run by the flamboyant Harry Hackney, it began as a clam stand in 1912 and grew into a huge restaurant. In 1926, "The World's Largest Seafood Restaurant" became a year-round establishment and it was expanded in 1929. Hackney's, frequented by celebrities, was famous for its lobster pool where you could choose your own. This postcard states that the seating capacity was "three thousand two hundred." It burned down in 1963, was rebuilt and reopened two years later, but closed permanently in the early 1980s.

Winter Modes. A catalog cover for Gimbel Brothers Department Store, Philadelphia, illustrates the latest fashions for the winter of 1926-27. Cold weather styles were as much a part of the Boardwalk "parade" as the summer fashions were as Atlantic City was as an all year attraction. Many of the visitors to the Jersey shore came from Philadelphia.

Stylish Strollers. In the 1920s, photographer Al Gold (left) takes a walk on the Atlantic City Boardwalk with his cousin Violet from Philadelphia and two unidentified friends. Gold would become Atlantic City's chief photographer from 1939 to 1964. *Vicki Gold Levi Collection.*

Knife and Fork Inn, Atlantic City, N. J.

218895

On the Menu. A c.1929 Hackneys menu cover reveals an insert with the "specials," some of which cost only $ 1.00 such as the "Assorted Sea Food Platter." It included "Fried Oysters, Fried Scallops, Deviled Clam, French Fried Potatoes, Hot Biscuits, Coffee, or Tea" *Hackney's menu cover and insert are from the Collection of Allen "Boo" Pergament.*

The Knife and Fork Rebellion. Established in 1912, the Flemish style Knife and Fork Inn's exterior is embellished with crossed knives and forks. It began as an exclusive Atlantic City gentlemen's club. During prohibition its members defied the law by openly serving liquor at their bar. It wasn't long before federal agents stormed the place and confiscated all the booze. The club's membership declined, and it was sold to the Latz family who removed the bar and converted the club into a quality restaurant. There were changes of ownership within the family over the years and it almost shut down in the 1990s, but in 2005, Frank Dougherty and his family purchased The Knife and Fork Inn. Dougherty, owner of Dock's Oyster House, another historic Atlantic City restaurant, has restored the inn to it's Roaring '20s grandeur. (*This postcard view is from 1916, but the exterior has remained much the same over its entire history.*)

ROSS FENTON FARM, ASBURY PARK, N. J.

Speakeasies? Everyone knew there were speakeasies all along the Jersey coast, even law officials, but they often looked the other way. Some were at restaurants or hotels and some were at private homes or clubs. Two establishments that served "tea" but reputedly offered more potent drinks were The Ross Fenton Farm in Wanamassa and Vivian Johnson's in Monmouth Beach. (Both of these restaurants are gone today.)

VIVIAN JOHNSON'S, OCEAN AVENUE, MONMOUTH BEACH, N. J.

Delectable Treats. Salt water taffy is sold at various Jersey shore resorts, but is usually associated with Atlantic City. Legend attributes the candy's origin to an Atlantic City Boardwalk shop owner, whose taffy got drenched in salt water during a storm in the 1880s, giving it a unique and delicious taste. The two most famous Atlantic City companies to make the famous treats are Fralinger's founded in 1885 and James, established in 1905. This colorful late '20s advertising brochure for Fralinger's depicted their store locations and listed the yummy flavors that were available.

Big Cast, Little Show! The cast of the 1929 musical revue, *The Little Show*, assembled on the Atlantic City Boardwalk in front of Nixon's Apollo Theatre for this panoramic portrait. The musical revue with words by Howard Dietz and music by Arthur Schwartz starred Clifton Webb, Fred Allen, and Libby Holman went to Broadway after its Atlantic City tryout. Besides the main subjects, backgrounds of old photos provide interesting information and the studio of Astrologer Prof. A.F. Seward looks quite intriguing. *Vicki Gold Levi Collection.*

Nixon's Apollo (a 1925 program cover). The premier Boardwalk theater at Atlantic City, it hosted tryouts for Broadway shows throughout the Roaring '20s. Well-to-do theatergoers from New York and Philadelphia attended the first nights and elegantly gowned ladies would make grand entrances, a tradition that continues at today's red carpet award shows. Besides musicals and operettas, a diverse variety of shows were presented including the innovative dancing of Ruth St. Denis and Ted Shawn, classical Shakespearean drama by Robert B. Mantell and Genevieve Hamper, and the baffling illusions of Thurston, the magician. Hundreds of top notch live shows were presented at the Apollo until the Depression when it even shut down for a season. Then, it was reopened as a movie house in 1934, went to burlesque, then to x-rated films in the 1970s, and eventually met the wrecking ball in 1985.

Pretty Ladies. The spectacular *Ziegfeld Follies* revues were tried out at the Apollo before opening on Broadway in New York as well as *George White's Scandals* (that also played at The Garden Pier) and other extravaganzas. Shown here are sheet music covers from the 1922 *Follies* and the 1926 *Scandals*.

"World's Most Famous Auditorium." A year or two before it officially opened in 1929, brochures began touting The Convention Hall designed by Lockwood, Green & Company Inc. of Boston. The enormous facility between Georgia and Mississippi Avenues was built by the City at a cost of $ 10,000,000. Convention Hall promoters claimed it could seat "the entire permanent population of Atlantic City -66,000- and still leave room to spare!" The main auditorium had removable seats and housed the largest organ in the world as well as a skating rink, ballroom, and more. In its early years, there were splendid flower shows as well as dog and horse shows. The Miss America Pageant was the main event here from the 1940s through 2004 (The pageant moved to Las Vegas.) and the hall hosted the Ice Capades, hockey games, the Democratic National Convention in 1964 and a huge Beatles concert also in 1964. (Details opposite page)

Strolling at Wildwood. Postmarked in 1921, this postcard of the Wildwood Boardwalk looking North from Maple Avenue, gives a look at the GEM 5, 10 & 25 cent store where strollers could buy novelties and souvenirs. Next to it is the Geo. E. Mousley Co. Roof Garden where they could then go for some delicious ice cream and soda.

Boardwalk Looking North from Maple Avenue, Wildwood, N. J.

Cedar Ave. Looking East towards Ocean, showing Whip and Jack Rabbit, Wildwood, N. J.

Staying Alive. A 1923 view of the Wildwood Boardwalk at "Cedar Ave., looking East towards Ocean, showing Whip and Jack Rabbit" has a message from Blanche to William. She says "Just a card to remind you that I am still living, and having a good time!" The Whip is easy to see on the right and the Jack Rabbit is the roller coaster visible in the background on the right.

The Matinee Line. – On the Ocean City boardwalk c.1929, children are waiting in a long line to see a movie at the Moorlyn Theater. The name of the film is not readable in the photo, but it was certainly a major attraction. ©*Ocean City Historical Museum, Inc.*

A Family Crowd. Men, women, and children are all looking at the camera person as they pause on the Ocean City Boardwalk at Ninth St. for this 1927 photograph. This was during the summer right before the terrible October fire that destroyed most of the Boardwalk. ©*Ocean City Historical Museum Inc.*

SCENE ON THE INLET, BAY HEAD, N. J.

A Quaint Movie House. A 1920s postcard of the inlet at Bay Head provides a lovely view of the little Lorraine movie theater, the small white building that is reflected in the water. Vacationers could see their favorite stars like Charlie Chaplin, Clara Bow, John Barrymore, and Mary Pickford in photoplays even at many of the small resort towns along the Jersey coast.

A Good Day for Ducks. Celebrated Jersey shore artist Dick LaBonté's 1982 painting, "A Rainy Day At The Seashore" depicts a children's matinee in the 1920s at The Lorraine theater in Bay Head. The movie playing, "Land of the Silver Fox" stars Rin Tin Tin, one of the most popular stars of the Roaring '20s! Alas, the theater is no longer there and the fun of sloshing through the puddles in boots and yellow slickers has been replaced by staying at home to watch DVDs. The well-loved artist, born in the '20s, lives in Bay Head. ©1982 Courtesy of LaBonté Prints, Inc.

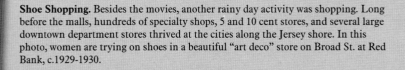

Shoe Shopping. Besides the movies, another rainy day activity was shopping. Long before the malls, hundreds of specialty shops, 5 and 10 cent stores, and several large downtown department stores thrived at the cities along the Jersey shore. In this photo, women are trying on shoes in a beautiful "art deco" store on Broad St. at Red Bank, c.1929-1930.

81

Barnegat Light   Barnegat City, N. J.

Sightseeing. Families visiting the Jersey shore in the Roaring 1920s enjoyed motoring along the coast to see the sights. Lighthouses are always of interest to tourists. This beautiful '20s Albertype postcard depicts the Barnegat Lighthouse, still a popular attraction today.

Dancing the Night Away. At the dance hall located on the end of the old Long Branch pier, these dancers and spectators look quite startled, perhaps by the flash bulb. Dance marathons were held here and at other resorts along the Jersey coast in which contestants would dance till they dropped, even for days, to win cash prizes. The marathon craze started in the mid '20s and continued through the early '30s.

A Family Souvenir. A stylish trio poses on the beach at Barnegat City (now Barnegat Light) with the lighthouse known as "Old Barney" in the background, c.1925. Evelyn Kinsey Thomas is in the dark hat and dress on the right standing next to Robert and Dorothy Thomas Bloomer. *Collection of Margaret Thomas Buchholz.*

TANGO ON THE BEACH, ATLANTIC CITY, N. J.

T-A-N-G-O. Originating in South America, the Tango became popular in the United States around 1914 and continued to be a favorite dance in the 1920s. On this postcard, couples are doing the Tango barefoot on the beach in Atlantic City for a crowd of Boardwalk onlookers. The sensual dance has been revived over the years and is well-liked at clubs and ballrooms today.

GARDEN PIER
BALL ROOM

DANCING
OVER THE
WAVES

"Dancing Over the Waves." This artist's depiction of the elegant "Garden Pier Ball Room" is from a 1922 promotional booklet for Atlantic City. Several of the ocean piers had ballrooms as well as the big hotels, and the popularity of dancing reached new heights. These well-heeled couples appear to be doing the Foxtrot, a dance that is still in favor with ballroom dancers.

The Latin Lover. Silent film idol of the Roaring '20s Rudolf Valentino (1895-1926) appeared in such classics as *The Sheik* and *The Four Horsemen of the Apocalypse* in which he performed his famous Tango scene. Italian-born Valentino spent time at Atlantic City and was even a dance instructor at the Garden Pier. He died from peritonitis at the age of 31, and over 100,000 fans, many of them hysterical women, lined up in New York City to view his casket.

Boardwalk Photography. Another favorite pastime at the Jersey shore resorts was having your portrait taken inside a professional photographer's studio. Tourists could choose various props and backdrops, the wicker rolling chair being the most popular. The pictures were usually made into postcards that the subjects could send to the folks back home. The photo of the woman alone is from Wildwood, the other three from Atlantic City. You might want to make up your own captions from the variety of expressions on their faces!

Mirror Images. These novelty photos were taken at the Dobkin Studio, 1517 Boardwalk, Atlantic City, next to the Apollo Hotel, c.1928. They are of the author's grandparents, Ruth H. and Dr. Melvin H., and her father, Douglas H. The vacationing family had their photos taken at Dobkin's from the 1920s through the 1930s.

Sports, Physical Culture, and Miscellany

After the First World War, the professional sports industry grew as people had more leisure time and more money to buy tickets for games. Arenas and stadiums were built as spectator sports became big business. Previously, it was mainly the aristocrats who indulged in sports and determined what games were in style. Their amateur athletic pursuits included lawn tennis, golf, trap shooting, boxing, horseback riding, polo and more. These activities were often conducted at their estates and summer homes such as those at the New Jersey shore. In the '20s, more working class people began to take up these leisure time activities that were once for the wealthy, especially golf and tennis.

Often called the "Golden Age of Sports," the 1920s saw the rise of great professionals who became legendary including baseball's Babe Ruth and football's Red Grange. In tennis, there was Big Bill Tilden, and golf had Bobby Jones. Boxing was perhaps the most popular spectator sport of them all in the Roaring '20s with the 1926 Jack Dempsey-Gene Tunney fight being one of the most memorable of the decade. Both professional and amateur sports excluded African Americans, but the Negro Leagues began during this decade and people started to take notice of talented black players.

Women gained recognition as competitive athletes. Along with the new morality, they were allowed to be more active and to wear clothes that gave them increased mobility. Gertrude Ederle, who summered and trained at the Jersey shore and became the first woman to swim the English Channel in 1926, helped to establish women in sports. Women golfers and tennis players became more competitive in both amateur and professional matches.

Outdoor activities such as boating, fishing, hunting, and trap shooting were all enjoyable pursuits during the era and people participated in them both for recreation and in competitions. Clubs, many of them exclusive, were established or expanded along the Jersey coast for these sports.

During the years of prohibition, an emphasis on health and exercise turned into an obsession. The physical fitness guru Bernarr Macfadden (1868-1955) was a major influence in the movement toward taking care of "the body beautiful." MacFadden, considered a kook by some, advocated rigorous exercise, natural foods, and alternative treatments for disease. Known as "the father of physical culture," Macfadden operated retreats for healthy living in New Jersey and elsewhere.

The postcards and photographs selected for this chapter, give a mere sampling of the wide scope of professional and amateur sporting events that took place at the Jersey Shore during the Roaring '20s. The illustrations also show how vacationers during those years of prohibition were into health and fitness, not so different from today.

In a Playful Mood. Heavyweight boxing champ Gene Tunney (1897-1978), trained at several of the numerous training camps that were in operation along the Jersey coast. Tunney, "The Fighting Marine," dethroned "The Manassas Mauler" Jack Dempsey (who trained at Atlantic City and other Jersey shore locations) in 1926 at Philadelphia. Some called it the fight of the century. Tunney was an advocate of healthy lifestyles and eventually proved to be quite an intellectual who lectured on Shakespeare. In this '20s image, obviously staged for publicity, an unidentified young sparring partner gives Tunney a jab with her left. *Collection of the Red Bank Public Library.*

Tunney and Walker. At the same unspecified New Jersey location as the previous photo, Gene Tunney (second from left) poses with trainers, a canine companion, and Mickey Walker, a boxer nicknamed "The Toy Bulldog" who hailed from Elizabeth New Jersey. (He is identified as the man on the far left next to Tunney.) Walker was a welterweight and middleweight champ who also proved himself as a golfer, a restaurateur, and an artist with his paintings even being exhibited at galleries. *Collection of the Red Bank Public Library.*

DeForest Training Camp. Some of the world's greatest pugilists including Jack Dempsey and Luis Firpo, "The Wild Bull of the Pampas." trained here under the famous boxing coach and instructor Jimmy DeForest. The camp, in operation from around 1900-1930, was located on the south side of Corlies Avenue (then Deal Beach Avenue). DeForest, aka James Woods, was originally a trapeze artist, a member of "The Flying DeForests." *Courtesy of Jane DeForest and The Township of Ocean Historical Museum.*

President Harding at Seaview. Dozens of upscale private golf courses dotted the Jersey coast in the Roaring '20s and one of the most prestigious of all was the Seaview County Club in Galloway Township, just across the bay from Atlantic City. Today it is the site of the modern Seaview Marriott Resort and golf course that retains its '20s charm. As the story goes, utility entrepreneur Clarence Geist became annoyed with long waiting times to tee off at the Atlantic City Golf Club (Northfield), so he decided to open his own club, Seaview, in 1912 where he entertained many notable guests. In this 1922 photo, Geist is on the far left next to President Warren G. Harding. New Jersey senator Joseph Frelinghuysen is on the other side of Harding and an unknown man is on the far right. The handsome Harding whose presidency was plagued with scandals, would die in office the year after this photo was taken. *Courtesy of Seaview Marriott Resort.*

Autographed photo of Warren Harding
Gift of Dr. and Mrs. Edward Dengrove

President Harding's Jersey Shore "Secret." Around the time of World War I, the dapper middle-aged Senator Warren G. Harding had a young mistress named Nan Britton who came from his Ohio hometown. In the summer of 1919, as he received the Republican nomination for president, she was pregnant with his child. Harding supporters helped Britton find a quiet place to await the birth. Asbury Park was her choice and at first she stayed at a hotel, but then moved to a modest but cozy house on Bond St. near Fifth Ave. and Sunset Park. On October 22, 1919, Elizabeth Ann was born at the house that still stands. She was delivered by Dr. J.F. Ackerman, "the society doctor of the Jersey shore." Her official birth certificate lists her father's name as "Edmund M. Christian" (the name of Harding's male secretary). Harding never saw his daughter though he gave financial support, and Britton moved to Chicago with the baby when she was about two months old. In 1921, Elizabeth Ann was adopted by Britton's sister and her husband. After Harding died in 1923, supposedly from tainted seafood (some people theorize that his wife poisoned him), there was no provision made for Britton and his illegitimate daughter. The Harding family refused to help them. Nan Britton wrote a "tell all" book, *The President's Daughter*, which was published in 1927. The 29th president's affair was no secret anymore. *Autographed original photo of President Harding and political buttons are from the collection of The Township of Ocean Museum.*

This unpretentious house in Asbury Park (as seen in 2008) is where President Harding's illegitimate daughter was born in 1919.

Hollywood Golf Club. Known as one of the finest golf clubs in the New York Metropolitan area for well over a century, the Hollywood Golf Club in Deal has an interesting history. Originally on the grounds of the Hollywood Hotel in Long Branch, it moved to the Norwood section of West Long Branch, and then to its current home on the former estate of George Washington Young and opera diva Madame Lillian Nordica. After World War I and its redesign by Walter J. Travis, the Hollywood Golf Club at Deal went through many changes. This photo is of the attractive 12th hole during the 1920s, "the golden age of golf." *Courtesy of Hollywood Golf Club.*

The 1921 Women's Amateur. Some high-spirited and talented women golfers competed in the national championship that was held at the Hollywood Golf Club with Marion Hollins (pictured here) taking the first place trophy. *Courtesy of Hollywood Golf Club.*

"Fore!" Alexa Stirling, the former women's amateur champ is demonstrating her swing. Though defeated by Hollis at the 1921 event at Hollywood, she was the first runner up. *Courtesy of Hollywood Golf Club.*

A Brit Golf Star. Cecil Leitch, a British golf champion, approaches the 10th green in the 1921 Women's Amateur. *Courtesy of Hollywood Golf Club.*

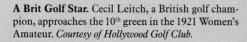

A Passageway. Two of the contestants at the 1921 Women's Amateur and a caddy pass through the charming tunnel leading from the 17th green to the 18th tee. *Courtesy of the Hollywood Golf Club.*

Mini Golf in a Small Town. The attractive little town of Loch Arbour, adjacent to Asbury Park, had its own miniature golf concession in the 1920s. It appears to be a simple course as many of them were when the game was still quite new. The first commercial-type mini course reportedly began at Pinehurst, NC, in 1916.

Boardwalk Golf. At Asbury Park, the miniature golf craze caught on quickly with courses located both on and off the boardwalk (that were less expensive). A 1929 photograph shows the "Obstacle Golf Course" at Fourth Ave. and Boardwalk, where it cost 25 cents to play the eighteen holes. The Berkeley Carteret hotel and the newly built Convention Hall are visible in the background.

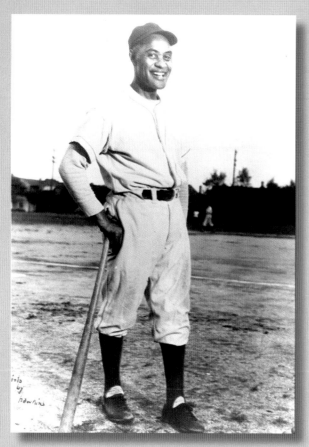

A Legendary Baseball Player. John Henry "Pop" Lloyd is not only regarded as the best shortstop to play in the Negro Leagues, but also as a scientific hitter, and a dedicated manager. "Pop" Lloyd, born in 1884 in Florida, belonged to quite a few teams during his Negro League career from 1906-1932. He is associated with Atlantic City history because he played with the Bacharach Giants of Atlantic City for the season of 1919, in 1922, from 1924-24, and retired after working with them again in 1931-32. On his retirement, Lloyd decided to make Atlantic City his home and continued playing semi-pro ball there until around 1942. He worked with young people and was an excellent role model. In 1949, a field at Indiana and Huron Avenues was dedicated to him. Pop Lloyd died in the mid 1960s and was posthumously inducted into the major league baseball Hall of Fame, Cooperstown, NY, in 1977. The Atlantic City field deteriorated as time went by, but thanks to the efforts of The John Henry "Pop" Lloyd Committee the Jersey shore ball field named for their hero was restored in the early 1990s. *Alfred M. Heston Collection, Atlantic City Free Public Library.*

BOARDWALK AND BEACH, SHOWING PHYSICAL CULTURE DRILL, ASBURY PARK, N. J.

Working Out at Asbury Park. In this postcard dated 1928, a large number of people are exercising on the Asbury Park beach as a crowd gathers on the Boardwalk to observe them. The instructor, in white slacks, stands on a platform in front of the class. Daily physical culture drills were commonplace at shore resorts in the Roaring '20s.

Anyone for Tennis? Looking smart and ready for the courts in their '20s tennis clothes, an unidentified amateur team of young women in Monmouth County pose for a portrait. Besides the outdated wooden racquets, observe their tennis shoes. They all have little heels except for one. Tennis, popular in the Roaring '20s, was played with wooden racquets that were still common until the 1980s.

Popular Reading. In 1899, fitness guru Bernarr MacFadden began to publish *Physical Culture* magazine that reached its height of popularity in the 1920s. His New York publishing house also produced well-read magazines including *True Story* and *Photoplay*.

An advertisement for a Turkish Bath in the Electric Building at Asbury Park, the Jersey Shore's only "skyscraper" in the 1920s.

Now Let's Stretch to the Right. The Ocean City beach during the 1920s was well known for its free daily physical culture classes that were supervised by Ward Beam (not the instructor in these photos) and sponsored by the city. In this 1925 photo, people of all ages are stretching on the 9th St. beach.. ©*Ocean City Historical Museum Inc.*

Bodies on the Beach! This photo was taken on the same morning in 1925 as the previous picture of the Ocean City exercise class. It appears that the group has been told to rest at the end of the class, or perhaps they merely taking a little break? The instructor seems to be the only one standing! ©*Ocean City Historical Museum Inc.*

Gertrude Ederle & her Trainer, Bill Burgess

"We're Waiting for You, Trudy"

Gertrude Ederle Welcome Home Celebration

Highlands, New Jersey

Tuesday, Aug. 31, 1926 at 3 P.M.

SWIMMING POOL FROM CASINO, DEAL, N. J.

A Stylish Pool. In this late 1920s postcard, a lone automobile is parked, perhaps with a chauffeur waiting to pick up a family member, at the Deal Casino swimming pool. The original casino built c.1906 was razed soon after a new one was built a few blocks north on Ocean Ave. in 1957. In the background are seen lovely summer "cottages" with manicured lawns.

A Female Swimming Star. A determined nineteen-year old athlete named Gertrude Ederle made headlines worldwide when she became the first woman to swim the treacherous English Channel in 1926. She was from New York City but her family summered at Highlands, NJ, where Trudy learned to swim. At first, her parents would hold her by a rope secured around her waist. When she was proficient, she trained by swimming the strong currents of the Shrewsbury River. In the 1924 Paris summer Olympic Games, she won one gold and two bronze medals. After swimming the English Channel, she was honored with a ticker tape parade in Manhattan, then a "welcome home" celebration at Highlands on August 31, 1926. On September 12, she appeared before a record crowd at Atlantic City's Steel Pier. Ederle played herself in a 1927 movie, *Swim Girl Swim*, and had a short-lived vaudeville career. She became a symbol of the growing recognition of women during the '20s, but her fame had diminished by the 1940s and she had lost her hearing. In 2000, "Gertrude Ederle Day" was held in Highlands to honor the swimming star at a park named for her. She died three years later in a New Jersey nursing home, at the age of ninety-eight. This 1926 photo is of Gertrude Ederle with her trainer Thomas Burgess who, in 1911, was the second man to swim the English Channel. (*Cover of program book is courtesy of Moss Archives*).

Hygeia Baths—Ocean and Pool Bathing, Hot and Cold Sea Water Tub Baths.
Rhode Island Avenue and Boardwalk, above Heinz's Pier, Atlantic City, N. J.
Open all year, Day and Night. Filtered water pumped constantly from Ocean.

"Open all year, Day and Night." Atlantic City's Hygeia Baths featuring this big heated swimming pool were located at Rhode Island Ave. and Boardwalk, above Heinz's Pier. Although this card is postmarked in November 1921, it appears to be the same view used for over a decade when it opened. The sender writes, "Here with 15 others for swim" (probably a team competition). As more and more hotels added their own swimming pools, the once bustling Hygeia Baths' business declined.

You can do it! At Ocean City's Flanders Hotel's salt water terrace pool, a coach with a megaphone encourages two swimmers. This photo dates to the 1920s, before the great fire of 1927. After that time, the boardwalk was moved closer to the ocean and a large pool complex was built in front of the Flanders, although this pool also remained in use.©*Ocean City Historical Museum Inc.*

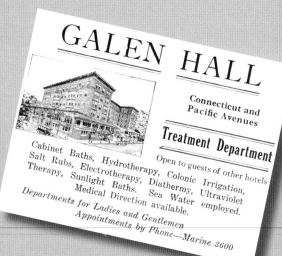

Spa Treatments. This 1927 ad is for Galen Hall, a large off-Boardwalk Atlantic City hotel at Connecticut and Pacific Aves. Their baths and health services were open to guests of other hotels.

Daily Doings, a 1929 promotional brochure printed in Allenhurst listed movie times, concerts, sporting events and religious services.

The Sporting Life. Just outside of Atlantic City and at many points along the coast, outdoors enthusiasts would fish and hunt. (*Page from a 1922 Atlantic City area promotional booklet.*)

A Fishy Story? Could this tuna caught at Manasquan Beach really weigh 1,800 lbs. as this postcard claims? According to some of today's fishermen, it's possible. All along the Jersey coast, fishing was both a sport and a source of income, although now there are more restrictions placed on what can be caught and what size can be kept than there were in the 1920s.

BOAT LANDING, ISLAND HEIGHTS, N. J.

Victorian Charm. A late 1920s postcard of the boat landing at Island Heights, near Toms River in Ocean County illustrates the tranquility of the small town. Founded in the 1870s by Methodists, it was unaffected by prohibition and remains dry to this day. The Philadelphia department store mogul John Wanamaker operated a training camp for his employees here in the early 20th century. A haven for both sportsmen and artists, Island Heights is a good place to enjoy fishing, sailing, or just relaxing.

Sitting on the Dock of the Bay. Three cute kids are having fun wasting time and fishing with a homemade pole. They are perched on the public dock on Barnegat Bay at 78th St., Harvey Cedars in the 1920s. The dock still exists, although it's been rebuilt several times. *Collection of Margaret Thomas Buchholz.*

A Labor Day Challenge. At Kinsey Cove in Harvey Cedars (LBI), the greased pole contest was an annual Labor Day event. Gutsy competitors would shimmy out on a slippery pole over the water vying to reach a prize such as a huge, delectable ham. Most everyone from town would gather round to watch. In this c.1928 photo, note the parked cars, the water tower, and the lone building in the center, a boat house that belonged to Frederick P. Small, president of American Express. *From "Seasons in the Sun: A Photographic History of Harvey Cedars, 1894-1947" by Margaret Thomas Buchholz, ©1994.*

Sneakbox Fun. In front of the Harvey Cedars' public dock looking north, the boys on the sneakbox are (left to right) Albert, Lester and Joseph L. Yearly. The girl is unidentified. This type of boat was originally used for duck hunting. *Photo by Joseph F. Yearly, courtesy of his granddaughter, Mary Flanangan.*

Original Belmar Yacht Club. A jaunty automobile is parked in front of the original Belmar Yacht Club on River and Eleventh Avenues on this c.1920 postcard. In 1928, a new club replaced this one at Oakwood and River Avenues, but is no longer in existence today. Both sailing and motor yachting were popular pastimes enjoyed during the 1920s.

A Yacht Club on the Bay. Located on Great Egg Harbor Bay and Inlet, the yacht club has a history dating to the late 19th century. In the background of this 1920s view is the old clubhouse, built in 1912, that was destroyed by the 1944 hurricane. The first floor with its billiard room and men's lockers was "off limits" to women but they were welcome at the Marine Grill and dance hall on the second floor.

PONIES IN FRONT OF MARLBOROUGH-BLENHEIM HOTEL, ATLANTIC CITY, N. J.

Equestrians and Observers. Riding on the beach was a sporting activity for well-heeled tourists at Atlantic City, especially in the Fall and Winter. This early '20s postcard depicts "Ponies in front of the Marlborough-Blenheim Hotel." Some African American youths who were apparently working as grooms for the horses can be seen on the right.

The Dashing Race Car Driver. Athletic and handsome, Wallace Reid was a matinee idol who played the role of a daredevil driver in many silent films. Automobile racing was a rapidly growing sport in America and a popular theme for movies. The child of theatrical parents, Reid grew up in Highlands, NJ. His family lived on Navesink Ave. and then on Portland Rd. in the Highlands Hills where an actor's colony thrived in the late 19th to early 20th century. This photo of Reid with Mary MacLaren is from *Across the Continent* (1922), one of his last films before his death at the age of thirty-one. In 1919, he took morphine prescribed for pain after he was in a train wreck and became addicted to it. There was no proper care for drug addiction and as his dependency increased, his physical health deteriorated. In 1923, he went into a coma after coming down with the flu and never recovered. He's remembered with a star on the Hollywood Walk of Fame.

Ponies on the Beach. This view near the Traymore Hotel in the late 1920s was obviously in cold weather judging by the coats worn by Boardwalk strollers and the lack of bathers on the beach.

A Sandy Bridle Path. Several children are riding ponies on the Atlantic City beach with two adult riders guiding them in 1921. The beauty of the waves makes the postcard scene look like a painting, as well as the fact that it is marked on back as "Phostint," a color process used by the Detroit Publishing Co. The sender writes about the ponies and how she is impressed by the Boardwalk that is "seven and one half miles long." She adds, "I think it is the only one like it in the world!"

ALL YEAR ROUND AT THE JERSEY SHORE

By the mid-1920s, much of the open land along the New Jersey coast was being transformed into housing developments. As if by the wave of a magic wand, houses appeared all over! A building boom occurred during the mid 1920s (and an even larger one in the 1950s after the Second World War). New Jersey shore towns that previously had large populations only in the summer, attracted year-round homeowners and city commuters. Farms and forests gave way to houses. Old hotels that once packed in summer guests made the transition to "residential" hotels. Rejecting the Victorian extended family system, many young families of the 1920s desired smaller houses with modern conveniences. More single people, leaving their family homes behind, looked for apartments.

Shark River Hills. A 1925 advertising giveaway fan (front and back shown here) gave statistics for "The New Asbury Park Suburb." The two postcards of Shark River Hills (Neptune Township) (opposite page) from the early '20s show the beauty of open land from "Sky Top." Houses were springing up all along the Monmouth County coast and much of the open land would soon be developed.

VIEW FROM SKY TOP, SHARK RIVER HILLS, N. J.

FROM SKY TOP CAN BE SEEN ASBURY PARK, OCEAN GROVE, SPRING LAKE AND THE ATLANTIC OCEAN.

VIEW IN MARVIN GARDENS, ATLANTIC CITY, N. J.

SKY TOP, SECOND HIGHEST POINT ON THE JERSEY COAST, SHARK RIVER HILLS, N. J.

How *Do* You Spell This Property? The residential neighborhood, "Marvin Gardens," is spelled incorrectly on this 1929 postcard, even before it gained fame as a property in Monopoly.™ For the legendary board game that was first sold in the early 1930s, the game's inventor, Charles Darrow, had misspelled it. The correct name of the attractive community south of Atlantic City is "Marven Gardens" derived from "MARgate" and "VENtnor." It is on the line that divides Margate City and Ventnor City. The development, built in the '20s, consists of homes in a variety of styles such as Dutch Colonial, English Tudor, and Spanish Colonial. Similar houses were being constructed in many towns at the Jersey shore during the decade.

COME TO FLORIDA!

The '20s real estate investments made at the New Jersey shore proved to be better deals than the "get rich quick" schemes involving properties in Florida. In those prosperous years of the Coolidge administration, Florida was being promoted as the glamorous place to vacation or live. Transportation was improving, and the Sunshine State looked like paradise. People jumped on the bandwagon to buy Florida land and a "speculative fever" took over. Many northerners lost their savings purchasing Florida lots, sight unseen, that turned out to be swamps fit only for alligators or beachfront property that was under water at high tide. The 1926 Miami hurricane contributed to the crash of the Florida land boom and prices dropped to only a few dollars per acre. It would take years before the development of Florida became a truly sound investment.

THE CRASH OF 1929

Besides land, Americans were buying stocks during the prosperous years of the 1920s. Stock prices rose to new heights during an unprecedented bull market. The investors included average people who bought stocks and then borrowed money to buy more. After all, they reasoned, automobile and electronics companies are reaping big profits these days, we can benefit too! As stock prices soared, even more people wanted to invest and speculation created an "economic bubble" that was bound to burst. And that's exactly what happened. On Thursday, October 24, 1929, the collapse of the stock market seemed unavoidable, things got worse on Monday and on Tuesday, the panic was full blown as speculators got rid of 16 million shares

on the market. Crowds gathered outside the New York Stock Exchange in disbelief on October 29, 1929, the day that would go down in history as "Black Tuesday." The crash was not the only cause, but it fueled the downward spiral that led to the Great Depression.

The grand adventure of the Roaring '20s was over for those blithe tourists in furs and expensive suits who strutted on the Boardwalk in Atlantic City. Gone were the happy-go-lucky days when the white-collar workers and raucous conventioneers acted out their fantasies while being waited on by others. Now, most everyone would be in much the same boat, looking for work and trying to make ends meet. Nevertheless, the Jersey shore survived during the Great Depression because people could not afford to go far away so they stayed close to home and enjoyed the local resorts. Moderately priced hotels and motels flourished and so did the ordinary restaurants, cafeterias, and diners that began at this time. Movies and sports events fared well and people went out for entertainment although home radio kept gaining in popularity.

Apartment Living. Built in 1928, Les Gertrudes apartments in Red Bank looks much the same in 2008. Located at the northeast corner of Broad St. and Pinckney Rd., the Spanish revival style building's units originally rented for about $95 to $150, not cheap for that period although it sounds incredible today. Apartments and residential hotels were becoming popular in the Roaring '20s.

THE REPEAL OF PROHIBITION

After almost fourteen years, on December 5, 1933, prohibition ended when Utah became the 35th state to ratify the 21st Amendment. "The Noble Experiment" simply didn't work. People who drank had continued to drink bootlegged liquor, crime had increased and the cost for the government to enforce the ban properly would have been astronomical. The repeal of prohibition was celebrated with headlines such as "Beer is Back" and breweries in cities including Newark, NJ, resumed business. At the New Jersey shore resorts, hotel and restaurant owners rejoiced as they opened up their bars and served wine with fine dinners. On the other hand, local boaters and fisherman who had been supplementing their income by bootlegging and the gangsters who thrived on the illegal trade were not quite so happy.

LES GERTRUDES APARTMENTS, RED BANK, N.J.

5175-29

THE SONG THAT NEVER ENDS

Understanding the lost world of our grandparents and parents requires respect and contemplation. Their lifestyle was "modern" to them but new technology is constantly altering the way we live. However, improvements in transportation and communications have not necessarily changed attitudes. Restrictions determined by race and religion at Jersey shore resorts have been alleviated over the years but are, in essence, not totally gone.

The freewheeling '20s generation who rejected Wilson's League of Nations as they rejoiced at the close of the "war to end all wars" would be confronted with another conflict before long. Their optimism would fade and the isolationism of the United States was one of the factors leading to World War II.

The Roaring '20s are legendary now. Although the New Jersey shore's year-round population has grown dramatically since the 1920s, summer crowds still visit. The coast has gone through many changes but people keep going to the beaches and breathing in the salt air and listening to the roar of the ocean…the roaring that never stops.

THE WHITE BORDER ERA

Most of the picture postcards produced from about 1915 to 1930 have thin white borders around the edges. The postcards representing the Roaring '20s featured in this book fall into that category. In the decade or so prior to this time a postcard "craze" had swept America dominated by exquisitely crafted cards made in Germany. During this so-called "Golden Age of Postcards" almost everyone sent greetings home from their vacations, mailed them for holidays or wrote them just to keep in touch.

With the outbreak of World War I, the German cards declined and more publishers in the United States began to manufacture cards. During the war, many European postcard businesses had been destroyed and afterwards high import taxes further contributed to their fall. American printers lacked experience in postcard manufacture and the cost of ink was said to be high. Consequently, the usual explanation for the white borders is that the printers wanted to economize and save ink. However, some collectors and historians believe that the white borders were made to simulate the borders that were around photographs. These postcards are considered "inferior" cards to earlier ones.

A few other types of postcards besides the typical white border ones were used during the 1920s and are represented in this book. The Albertype Company of Brooklyn, New York, produced a lovely soft tinted style without borders. "Real photo" postcards made on photographic paper, were mostly portraits taken in studios at resorts that were popular with tourists as they had been in prior years.

Postcard use declined in the 1920s possibly due to technology as people found that they could phone home more easily than sitting down to write a card. Amateur photography kept gaining in popularity and small format family photos replaced many postcards of previous years. Professional photographers' equipment kept improving with better exposure times and outdoor photography reached new heights.

The white border cards, though produced in abundance, are rapidly becoming scarcer and provide an important record of their time. They are often the only surviving evidence of a certain building, scene event, pastime, or fashion trend of the Roaring '20s. In the early 1930s, the white border cards were replaced by brightly colored linen cards that had a high rag content. "The Linen Card Era" was then replaced by the "Modern Photochrome Era" with bright, sharp chrome cards starting around 1939 and marketed to the present day.

A white border 1924 Atlantic City postcard.

A 1929 "Greetings from Belmar" white border postcard.

A 1925 Asbury Park and Ocean Grove souvenir postcard folder.

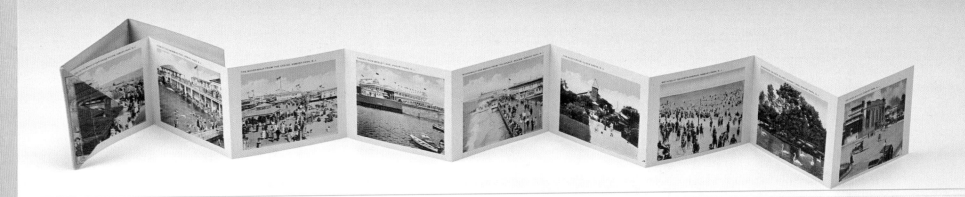

Selected Bibliography

Allen, Frederick Lewis. *Only Yesterday, An Informal History of the 1920s*. New York: Harper & Row, 1931.

Atlantic City, The World's Playground. National City Publicity Company, May, 1922.

Buchholz, Margaret Thomas, Ed., *Shore Chronicles*. Harvey Cedars, NJ: Down The Shore Publishing, 2003.

Buchholz, Margaret Thomas, and Savadove, Larry. *Island Album, Photographs and Memories of Long Beach Island*. Harvey Cedars, NJ: Down the Shore Publishing, 2006.

Cunningham, John T. and Cole, Kenneth D., *Atlantic City*. Charleston, SC: Arcadia Publishing, 2000.

Gabrielan, Randall. *Long Branch, People and Places*. Charleston, SC: Arcadia Publishing, 1998.

Kent, Bill, with Ruffolo, Robert E. Jr. & Dobbins, Lauralee. *Atlantic City, America's Playground*. Encinitas, CA: Heritage Media Corp., 1998.

LaBonté, Dick. *Paintings of the Jersey Shore and More*. Bay Head, NJ: Jersey Shore Publications, 2002.

Levi, Vicki Gold, & Eisenberg, Lee. *Atlantic City, 125 Years of Ocean Madness*. Berkeley, California: Ten Speed Press, 1979.

Lloyd, John Bailey. *Eighteen Miles of History on Long Beach Island*. Harvey Cedars, NJ: Down the Shore Publishing, 1994.

McMahon, William. *So Young...So Gay! Story of the Boardwalk 1870-1970*. An Atlantic City Press Publication, 1970.

Pike, Helen-Chantal. *Greetings from New Jersey, A Postcard Tour of the Garden State*. New Brunswick, NJ: Rutgers University Press, 2001.

Pike, Helen-Chantal. *Asbury Park's Glory Days, The Story of an American Resort*. New Brunswick, NJ: Rutgers University Press, 2005.

Roberts, Russell and Youmans, Rich. *Down the Jersey Shore*. New Brunswick, NJ: Rutgers University Press, 1993.

Simon, Bryant. *Boardwalk of Dreams, Atlantic City and the Fate of Urban America*. New York: Oxford University Press, 2004.

"The "Roaring '20s," The Township of Ocean Museum, exhibit, 2006.

Walzer, Jim and Wilk, Tom. *Tales of South Jersey, Profiles and Personalities*, New Brunswick, NJ: Rutgers University Press, 2001.

Wilson, Harold F. *The Story of the Jersey Shore*. Princeton, NJ: D. Van Nostrand Company, Inc., 1964.

Periodicals
Asbury Park Press
Atlantic City Weekly (especially "Waltz Through Time" columns by Jim Waltzer)
Atlantic City Press (The)
Hub (The)
Long Branch Record
New Jersey Monthly
New York Times (The)
Red Bank Daily Register
Trenton Times (The)

Internet
www.anchorandpalette.com for more information about the work of Jersey shore artist Dick LaBonté.

http://library.duke.edu/digitalcollections/eaa/. "RC Maxwell Collection, Emergence of Advertising On-Line Project," John W. Hartman Center for Sales Advertising & Marketing History, Duke University Rare Book, Manuscript, and Special Collections Library

INDEX OF PLACES

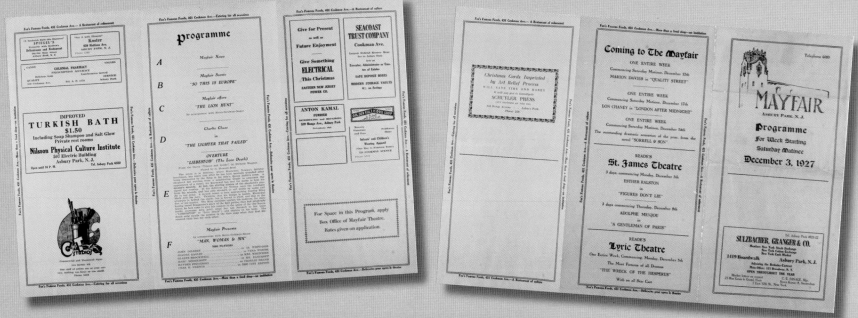

Movie Program. The exquisite Spanish Mission Revival style Mayfair Theater at Asbury Park opened in 1927, was demolished in 1974, but is not forgotten. Located beside Wesley Lake, it was a popular venue for both movies and vaudeville. The back of this December 1927 Mayfair program lists what was playing at the other Reade's Asbury Park theaters (none of them in existence today).

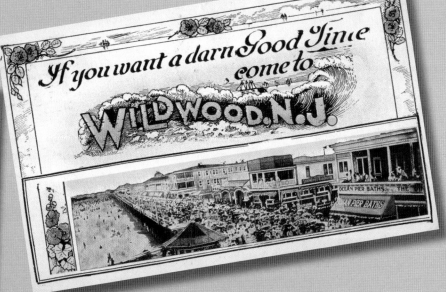

Amusing Greetings. This pair of humorous postcards were both postmarked Aug. 4, 1922, from Wildwood and mailed to the same person in Punxsutawney, PA, but from two different senders.